PRACTICAL
BARBEL FISHING

Graham Marsden and Mark Wintle

PRACTICAL
BARBEL FISHING

Graham Marsden and Mark Wintle

The Crowood Press

First published in 2010 by
The Crowood Press Ltd
Ramsbury, Marlborough
Wiltshire SN8 2HR

www.crowood.com

British Library Cataloguing-in-Publication Data
A catalogue record for this book is available from the British Library.

ISBN 978 1 84797 203 3

Acknowledgements
We would like to thank the following for their assistance in compiling
this book: Pete Reading and John Searl.

Typeset by Jean Cussons Typesetting, Diss, Norfolk

Printed and bound in China by Leo Paper Products

CONTENTS

PREFACE

There may come a time in the not-too-distant future when barbel are found in as wide a variety of waters as carp; for now, however, they are largely confined to most of the rivers in England and Wales. A few stillwaters have been stocked with the species and the fish seem to be thriving – but barbel, predominantly a river fish, in stillwater remains a controversial topic (of which more later).

Like carp, barbel have become something of a cult species (hence the controversy regarding stillwaters), and their popularity grows with each passing year. That is not surprising, for the barbel is a well built, powerful fish that, pound for pound, fights as well as, if not better than, any other coarse fish. And that is exactly what the majority of specialist coarse anglers want: a fish that puts a proper bend in the rod.

Unlike most coarse fish, barbel are most often fished for straight off the rod top – that is to say, there is rarely any form of indicator to signal a bite before the rod comes into play. Bite indication is watching for a bend in the rod tip or, less often, quivertip – and this makes a massive difference to the adrenalin flow. You can be sat there, watching the rod tip, a slight bend in it and quivering slightly in the current … your thoughts drift away to who won the footy last Saturday, and then – bang! The rod tip takes a dive for the river, and the rod bends to a full fighting curve before you can even curl a tighter grip on the butt: the fight is on before you realize it, and it's a white-knuckle ride all the way to the landing net. And it is this, more than anything, which makes barbel fishing one of the most thrilling forms of coarse angling.

This book is aimed at filling that gap between the beginner to barbel angling, and the out-and-out advanced barbel angling specialist. It will steer you from beginner, through intermediate, right up to advanced standard in easy-to-understand, practical steps. It will tell you all about the barbel – its general behaviour and feeding habits – guide you to the best rivers, indicate the size of fish you are likely to catch in each river, describe and recommend the tackle, rigs and bait you need, and describe in depth the various methods needed to put the landing net under these wonderful fish. It will discuss short sessions and longer campaigns, delve into baiting strategies, cover stalking numerous swims and staying put in a single swim. And most importantly, it will help you put all the pieces of the jigsaw together so you can see the bigger picture for yourself.

Graham Marsden

INTRODUCTION

Slim, strong, muscular, and with the fighting prowess of a pit bull terrier: when it comes to barbel, this is a pretty accurate description – they really *are* built like that and fight like that, and it is mainly for this reason that they are such a popular species. Although many anglers are happy to get a few bites when they go fishing and pull in a succession of small roach, the more ambitious angler likes nothing better than to see his rod hooped over to a degree where the cork handle of the rod creaks beneath his fingers and line is ripped uncompromisingly from the reel. Nor is barbel fishing for the faint-hearted: it is for those who, like many anglers, want to outwit a crafty fish, but then to battle with that fish for several minutes at least until it is subdued enough to be pulled over the rim of a landing net.

Carp fishing provides a similar challenge and the same hard fight, but the difference with barbel fishing is that very often – in fact, most often – when the biggest fish are being targeted, it is a solitary, very individual confrontation, where a lone angler can often be found on a deserted stretch of river. Rather than the huge array of tackle the carp angler carries, the barbel angler will have just a small rucksack with a tackle box and a modest selection of baits. As often as not he carries one rod and reel and a single rod rest, and relies solely on seeing the rod top being punched over with sandbag force when a barbel takes the bait.

Nor does a barbel angler sit in a bivvy waiting for the bite alarms to warn him that he has a run on one of his battery of rods: barbel fishing is more to do with sitting on a low chair next to one or two rods propped on rod rests and pointing skywards, like centurions on silent vigil. The barbel angler is always aware that the peace could be shattered at any moment when one of the rods lurches over with alarming suddenness, and he has to dive into action to prevent the rod

Fishing at its best; success with a smile!

from hurtling into the river with frightening speed.

This isn't always the case, though, because now we have a growing band of barbel anglers who tackle the species with a carp-fishing approach, using carp rods, reels and heavier lines, rod pods and bite alarms, and who often bivvy up on the river. It's an approach more appropriate to big rivers such as the tidal Trent, and it has become so popular that it now has a name to describe it: 'carbelling', a hybrid of carp and barbel fishing. This book will cover carbelling for those who decide that this approach is the best one for them.

Apart from the heavy sit-and-wait approach of carbelling, barbel fishing owes a lot to the carp angler, for many of the rigs and baits the barbel angler uses were first introduced by carp anglers: the hair and bolt rig, boilies and pellets, for instance. The rigs and baits are often identical, but equally as often they are modified in some way to specifically suit barbel, particularly

when it comes to flavours, or at least in as much as the angler believes. Probably the real difference for the conventional barbel angler, rather than the carbeller, lies in the requirements, methods and means behind swim choice – and, of course, contending with flowing water rather than stillwater.

To a much lesser degree than carp fishing, barbel fishing has become an entity in its own right, separate to a degree from other coarse fishing. There are barbel-fishing organizations and one or two dedicated web sites, but as yet no nationally available magazines dedicated to the species. If big barbel were more widely available in more stillwaters, their popularity as a species would increase dramatically, but as yet that hasn't happened, and it is much to the relief of the barbel fanatics who see stillwater barbel as aliens in that environment. This will be discussed further in the book.

Barbel are not regarded as a particularly difficult species to catch once you have found the area where they are browsing, either feeding or between meals, so to speak – although where bigger barbel are concerned, on stretches that come under a great deal of angling pressure, the difficulty increases and it is the canny angler with a few tricks up his sleeve who defies the odds. This book will cover all the 'tricks', whether in relation to location, method or bait, and will help you to work out which trick or tricks could provide the answer.

Very often the problem isn't so much to do with tempting a bite and hooking a barbel as it is with landing one, for in certain swims the barbel are bold and fearless and will accept a bait simply because they feel safe in an area that offers them sanctuary, with bolt holes they can dive into and escape being captured by breaking the tackle or shedding the hook. Dense snags such as sunken branches and tree roots are the usual sanctuaries, and we discuss in depth the techniques for extracting barbel from such tackle-testing snags.

Fishing flooded rivers is another topic that will be dealt with in great depth, especially as it

A hard-fighting barbel tests your tackle to its limits.

is a known fact that barbel feed at their best in coloured water following a sudden influx of prolonged heavy rainfall. Fishing a flooded river can be a daunting experience for those who have never tackled one before; the sheer speed of the current, the debris that comes rushing down, snagging lines and burying hookbaits, all need to be dealt with using the right tackle and bait – and most of all, with the right attitude, for floodwater fishing demands a confident, positive approach.

Winter barbel fishing, although not as consistent as barbelling in the warmer months, usually produces the biggest fish as it is in winter that the barbel are at their fittest and fattest. This book will provide the answers to any questions you may have about barbel fishing in the cold winter temperatures.

Motivation, location, conditions, method, feeding, stalking, rigs and baits and much, much more, all come under the microscope in this practical and detailed guide to barbel fishing. You'll learn how to tackle running water and how to catch one of the hardest fighting fish in UK waters.

Glorious scenery is a bonus when barbel fishing, like this scenic part of the Dorset Stour.

1 ABOUT BARBEL

The barbel's streamlined shape, powerful muscles and strong mouth and barbules all indicate a fish that is highly adapted to living in fast, powerful rivers. The ideal barbel environment is considered to be a river of medium size with strong currents and great tresses of ranunculus swaying in the flow over clean gravel. Indeed, the barbel is so typical of this river environment that scientists call this section of the river 'the barbel zone'. Upstream of this zone the water is shallower and faster, and is where we would expect to find trout and grayling; further downstream the river steadies and widens and becomes suitable for bream, hence 'the bream zone'.

One of the attractions of barbel fishing is that not only are you fishing for a highly attractive fish, there is the added bonus that you are often doing so in highly attractive surroundings.

Barbel Lifestyle

Through the Seasons

The barbel is one of the last coarse fish to spawn, usually leaving the ritual until late May or early June, but if the latter days of spring are colder than usual then this can be delayed as late as the second half of June or even early July. When they do feel compelled to spawn they usually migrate upstream, where this is possible, to spawn on shallow gravelly areas. For the angler, this means that the barbel is often a slow starter, for they may not even be present in the usual swims – it doesn't mean that you can't catch barbel straight from the opening day of a new river season, but that sport could be patchy and you may have to look for different swims than those you usually fish as the season matures. Sport becomes more reliable in the

The glorious River Wye, full of barbel fishing promise.

RIGHT: *Ideal conditions in early September on the Dorset Stour: the level is up, the water is coloured – it's time to go barbel fishing!*

BELOW: *It may be midwinter, but there are days when the barbel are feeding.*

second half of July, and increasingly better in most years as autumn approaches, with late September, October and November being when they are at their best. Many barbel anglers prefer to wait a month or so after a new season opens to start their quest in earnest, and look forward to the cream of the sport later in the year.

One of the occasional pitfalls of summer conditions is low water, which can make the barbel especially wary. Conversely, a moderate summer flood can provide the best barbel fishing conditions of all, especially if a succession of moderate floods flushes out the usual summer flotsam and jetsam from the river and the ditches and backwaters that feed it.

Autumn tends to bring with it the first frosts and floods. The river weed that died back in late summer has rotted and lost its strength, and November floods clear the rivers of this summer weed growth. Water temperatures are dropping, too. Given the right conditions the barbel will still feed, but sport can be more hit or miss, especially with the first significant drop in temperature from a succession of frosts.

Winter can be a good time for barbel fishing, once the water temperature has settled to the winter norm and the barbel have become used to it. The good thing about winter is that it is possible to predict when barbel will be caught, for even a slight rise in temperature is often enough to trigger a feeding spell, even though it may be short-lived. A water temperature of

around 44°F (6.6°C) seems to be significant, with barbel being more inclined to feed when the water temperature climbs higher than this. The chances of catching barbel are best following a flood that warms the water, and at their worst when the river grows colder with snow melt or following a heavy frost. The lowest temperature at which barbel are likely to feed is 39°F (4°C): at this point feeding is spasmodic at best, with the barbel likely to be inactive, though just about still catchable if you manage to choose the right swim and drop a bait right under their nose.

A number of dedicated barbel anglers only fish through the winter, usually beginning an hour or so before dusk and fishing for three or four hours into darkness, which is the peak time

for barbel to feed on many rivers. The main motivation for fishing through winter is that the biggest barbel are usually at their best and heaviest, with each flood boosting their weights for a spell. If you wish to catch the biggest barbel in a river when they are at their heaviest weight, then you cannot ignore fishing for them in winter.

How Barbel Feed

It doesn't take more than a second glance at a barbel's head to get some idea about its feeding habits. Those four long and sensitive barbules that give it its name provide an excellent means of seeking out food from the riverbed, and its tough mouth is suited to sifting through fine gravel and nudging larger gravel and even sizable rocks out of the way to find food lurking underneath. The natural foods for barbel are very much the sort of creatures that do lurk under stones, such as caddis grubs, stonefly larvae, bullheads and loach, so they are well adapted to this sort of feeding behaviour. When we feed a swim with masses of particles such as hemp, maggots, casters or tiny trout pellets, these get washed down into the crevices between the gravel and stones on the riverbed, which is where barbel expect to find their food. This can trigger active foraging, which is ideal for catching shoal barbel. This active foraging often follows a pattern. The barbel start

at the downstream end of the baited area and work upstream until they sense nothing in the way of food, at which point they turn sharply and drop downstream to rejoin the back of the shoal to work upstream again. This behaviour is one reason for the classic smash-round barbel bite that is often preceded by a tentative knock or two.

One aspect of barbel feeding that has been long recognized is that of preoccupation. It can take a while for barbel to recognize a new food source as worth eating, but if enough people chuck enough in, then eventually the barbel in that water will become switched on to that bait to the exclusion of others. Examples of this abound, especially on heavily fished stretches of river. The Royalty Fishery on the Hampshire Avon at Christchurch in Dorset has been the scene of a number of periods where a particular bait dominated barbel fishing. The most noteworthy was the maggot era, to the point where the fishery management became so concerned about the adverse effect on other fish, notably sea trout, that they banned the use of maggots. Before this, Edam cheese had been the most popular bait. At nearby Throop on the Dorset Stour the dominant bait was hempseed, until that, too, was banned. In both cases, the bait bans were lifted many years later. Today the dominant barbel baits are pellets and boilies,

One of the classic barbel rivers, the River Swale.

but thankfully not to the exclusion of many other baits.

Distribution

Despite there being many sections of river in the UK which might be thought to provide the ideal habitat for barbel, the natural distribution of barbel in the UK was in fact much constrained by the massive upheaval of the last ice age about ten thousand years ago, and only those major river systems that connected to the mighty Rhine system ended up with a natural stock of barbel – and even then, some rivers, particularly the slower fenland rivers, missed out. That left only a handful of those rivers flowing into the sea on the eastern side of England holding barbel, namely the Trent and its tributaries, the Yorkshire rivers that joined the Humber, and the Thames and its tributaries.

Furthermore the industrial revolution, with its attendant pollution, destroyed the potential for some rivers to hold any fish, never mind barbel, and it was only from the 1980s onwards when the pollution problem was finally resolved that barbel returned to rivers such as the upper Trent and Don. There is an element of mystery as to whether the Great Ouse had a natural stock of barbel. There are a few catch reports prior to 1950 that suggest their natural presence, though with very few anglers targeting them the barbel remained generally undiscovered. There were certainly introductions of barbel from the 1950s onwards, and anglers such as Dick Walker and Ian Howcroft caught them at this time.

The first documented stocking of barbel is much earlier, going back to several stockings by Tommy Gomm in the late 1880s through to the early 1900s. Gomm introduced a consignment of Thames barbel to the Dorset Stour at Iford Bridge, just below the Throop Fishery, and possibly to the lowest reach of the Avon, best known as the Royalty Fishery – though we need to be careful here, because not just the Avon part of the river is technically known as the Royalty, it also includes the lowest section of the Stour. What we do know is that within two decades barbel became established in both the

Tackle and attitudes have changed and the barbel are bigger, but the enthusiasm has never waned.

Dorset Stour and the Hampshire Avon. Much later, further introductions led to the spread of barbel upstream on both rivers, though they have yet to become really established on the upper Stour despite several stockings in recent years. From these early stockings, both rivers became famous for their barbel fishing and for a long time represented the best chance of a double-figure fish.

An opportunity offered to *Angling Times* in 1955 represents the next big leap in barbel distribution: the owner of a Berkshire trout water (thought to be the Enbourne) offered the water's coarse fish, including numerous barbel, for restocking purposes, and in 1955 and 1956 *Angling Times* distributed these to the Severn, the Bristol Avon, the Trent and the Welland. The Severn was a heaven-sent opportunity for barbel, as the middle reaches from Stourport upstream to Shrewsbury were apparently ideal barbel habitat – and so it proved. Within a decade the original 500 barbel were breeding well and spreading both up- and downstream. The 1971 All England Championship on the middle Severn demonstrated just how well the barbel had thrived, the match being dubbed the 'barbel national', with many hefty catches being recorded at the weigh-in.

In the decades that followed, both legal and illegal introductions encouraged the spread of barbel. Two illegal introductions were to the River Ribble and the River Wye, though it is possible that a legal introduction to the Wye tributary, the Lugg, somewhat enhanced the stocking of the Wye. Legally, barbel were introduced to rivers as diverse as the Medway in Kent (1959), the Wensum in Norfolk and the Dane in Cheshire. Later, the Severn-Trent area of the NRA (later EA) developed a huge fish farm at Calverton in Nottinghamshire, and this concern has bred many millions of barbel, which they have distributed to waters all over the country. These young barbel have strengthened existing stocks where recruitment is low, and have provided a breeding nucleus for new rivers. Include further illegal introductions, and the list of rivers now holding barbel is considerable; even unlikely rivers such as the Exe and Itchen now hold barbel.

Barbel Size

For many decades the barbel record was unbeaten at 14lb 6oz, with three fish jointly holding the record; then in 1968 the BRFC threw out the old records, eventually accepting Joe Day's 1962 13lb 12oz Royalty fish as the new record. Later, the discovery of the cased body of the Honourable Almer Tryon's 14lb 6oz Royalty fish, one of the records that had earlier been thrown out, led to a campaign to reinstate it, and this was achieved in 1990.

UK Barbel Rivers

This list of UK barbel rivers indicates the extent of the spread of barbel; inevitably it will change over time due to new stockings. It does not include the side streams of larger rivers.

Southern England
Hants Avon, Dorset Stour, Moors, Bristol Avon, Somerset Frome, Marden, Itchen, Test, Sussex Ouse, Arun, Rother (Sussex), Medway, Kent Stour, Loxely, Sheaf

East Anglia/Wash
Great Ouse, Nene, Wensum, Welland, Witham, Ousel, Waveney, Yare, Ivel

Wales/WestMidlands
Wye, Lugg, Taff, Usk, Ely, Severn, Teme, Warks Avon, Warks Stour, Leam, Arrow, Salwarpe, Worfe, Vyrnwy

Trent/Notts/Staffs/Derbyshire
Trent, Tame, Sow, Derwent (Derbys), Anker, Mease, Soar, Dove, Wreake, Erewash, Leen, Penk, River Idle, Maun, Meden and Ryton

Thames
Thames, Evenlode, Windrush, Kennet, Thame, Cherwell, Lea, Ember, Mole, Blackwater, Colne, Colnebrook, Loddon, Wey, Ray, Wandle, Whitewater, Ray (Swindon), Frays

Yorks
Ouse, Don, Nidd, Wharfe, Swale, Ure, Derwent, Dearne, Calder, Aire, Rother

North East
Tees, Wear, Tyne

North West
Alder (Lancs), Dee, Alyn. Worthenbury Brook, Mersey, Tame, Etherow, Bollin, Goyt, Weaver, Croal, Bradshore Brook, Irwell, Peover Eye, Dane, Ribble

Scotland
Clyde, Avon (Scotland)

Barbel Records

Year	Captor	Venue	Weight (lb-oz-drs)
1888	T. Wheeler	Thames	14-06-00
1934	Almer Tryon	Hants Avon	14-06-00
1937	F. W. K. Wallis	Hants Avon	14-06-00

All the above were dropped in 1968 due to the BRFC list revision but the Tryon fish was reinstated in 1990.

Year	Captor	Venue	Weight (lb-oz-drs)
1962	Joe Day	Hants Avon	13-12-00
1987	Martin Hooper	Dorset Stour	14-02-00
1992	David Williams	Medway	14-06-00
1992	David Williams	Hants Avon	14-06-08
1992	David Taylor	Medway	14-09-00
1992	David Taylor	Medway	14-13-00
1993	Bob Morris	Medway	15-07-00
1993	Andy Harman	Medway	15-11-00
1994	Pete Woodhouse	Medway	16-02-00
1997	Howard Maddocks	Severn	16-03-00
1998	Stephen Keer	Wensum	16-06-00
1998	Dave Currell	Great Ouse	16-11-00
1999	Martin Bowler	Great Ouse	16-12-00
1999	Kevin Newton	Great Ouse	17-01-00
1999	Ray Walton	Great Ouse	17-04-00
2000	Guy Robb	Great Ouse	17-06-12
2000	Stuart Morgan	Great Ouse	17-09-00
2000	Stuart Morgan	Great Ouse	17-14-00
2001	Tony Gibson	Great Ouse	19-00-00
2001	Steve Curtin	Great Ouse	19-06-08
2004	Tony Gibson	Great Ouse	20-06-00
2006	Grahame King	Great Ouse	21-01-00

However, apart from the occasional monster, such as Charles Cassey's foulhooked Ibsley (Hants Avon) fish of over 16lb caught in the early 1960s, there was little real evidence that barbel could get much bigger than about 14lb. It is true that Dick Walker and others claimed to have seen 20lb monsters in the Avon in the 1960s, but with no evidence to support the claims, such fish remained the stuff of dreams.

The early 1990s heralded the start of a new era as far as rewriting the record books was concerned, and a succession of Medway fish raised the record from 14lb 6oz to 16lb 2oz during 1992 to 1994. Then first the Severn, followed by the Wensum, held the record, again with 16lb fish. The Wensum's hold on the record was tenuous, however, and a succession of Great Ouse fish has since carried the record from a high 16lb to more than 21lb. Initially the full list of record fish may give the impression of many different gigantic barbel, whereas what was actually happening was that the same fish are being recaptured at ever-increasing weights. These 'named' barbel were 'Red Belly' and 'The Traveller', and they accounted for the record several times (*see* table above).

Indeed, if we look at typical barbel catches from the 1960s, 1970s and 1980s, we quickly notice two things. First, there the average size of

This is the current British record barbel of 21lb 1oz, held by the captor Grahame King. (Courtesy of Grahame King)

barbel is comparatively small. On many waters anglers were catching barbel that averaged two or three pounds with even a seven-pounder an exceptional fish. For a realistic chance of a double-figure barbel, just about the only water was the Royalty Fishery on the Avon. It is true that some other waters did produce fish of this size, such as nearby Throop and a small Thames sidestream called the Potts Stream in Oxford, but these were rare exceptions. On parts of the Kennet and Lea, for example, there were shoals of small barbel. With the relatively small size of fish, the approach was to use tackle not that much stronger than roach tackle of the time, safe in the knowledge that nothing very big would turn up. Rods such as the Kennet Perfection, a 'light' version of the classic Avon, were teamed with 3–4lb line, making for exciting sport with barbel of 3–4lb but little match for a double-figure fish. So the first key point is that where barbel did occur they

were likely to be prolific, small and slow-growing.

A casual glance at big barbel pictures from these far-off days quickly tells you another fact. Even when barbel did get big they did not carry the weight that modern barbel do, and very few measure more than around 32in (81cm) in length. In past decades, barbel of 30–32in (76–81cm) would weigh around 10–12lb, possibly slightly more. Keen barbel anglers who have measured the girth of barbel over the decades have found there has been a steady increase in the girth of barbel. Look at pictures from the 1960s and 1970s, and many barbel from the past look scrawny by today's standards. There are several reasons for this; first, the colder winters of the 1960s and 1970s shortened the effective growing season, something that has altered in recent years and increased the average and ultimate size of many species.

Second, a parasitic hookworm (*pomporynchus laevis*) was endemic in fish in waters where there was heavy weed cutting, as on the Hampshire Avon. This orange, maggot-like grub used freshwater shrimps and snails as intermediate host. When the chub and barbel ate the infected shrimps and snails, the parasites developed and attached themselves to the gut of the fish. A chub or barbel could be host to hundreds of these hookworms. The draconian weed cutting of that time made these shrimps easily available to the fish. Dick Walker highlighted these emaciated fish. Fish that should have weighed 5lb struggled to make 3lb.

The other reasons are likely to be more obscure; increased competition for food is likely to be one reason, habitat damage due to dredging, which was far more extensive in the decades after World War II than more recently, and finally pollution in various forms.

In the last decade a further change has occurred. Not only are barbel much heavier for their length, but they are reaching a much greater ultimate size. This phenomenon is widespread. On many rivers barbel seem fewer yet much bigger. On numerous rivers the situation has changed from one where the average shoal barbel were, say, 5–7lb with the occasional eight- or nine-pounder and an outside chance of a double, to one where there is an even chance of a double. And with some of the biggest fish no longer weighing 11 or 12lb but well into the teens of pounds, it is hardly surprising that so many river records are being broken. Whether this is a bubble waiting to burst remains to be seen, but many barbel anglers have concerns over the lack of smaller barbel coming through to take the place of these big old fish. However, restocking and habitat restoration are addressing this situation, although other factors come into play.

Dredging is rare on the Dorset Stour nowadays, but the river suffered enormous damage from the 1940s to the 1980s.

ABOVE: The middle Severn proved to be the ideal habitat for barbel when they were transferred there more than fifty years ago.

BELOW: The Teme, a tributary of the Severn, is an excellent barbel river, as shown by this nine-pounder caught by Paul Williams.

Barbel that grow slowly tend to live much longer than those that grow much more quickly. Thus it has been found that barbel living in some cold northern rivers have reached the ripe old age of thirty, and exceptionally forty years. Faster-growing barbel are less likely to live so long.

Predation

When barbel are small they are likely to be preyed upon by the usual predatory fish – pike, perch, chub – and birds such as herons, cormorants and kingfishers. It is not surprising that when small, barbel spend most of their time among weedbeds, out of sight. When much bigger they are less prone to predation. Two

threats do exist; on waters very near the sea, occasionally a seal or two will visit and cause havoc among the barbel. This has happened on the tidal Ribble and the Royalty (which is also partly tidal) in the past.

A much more recent and widespread threat has come about from the reintroduction of otters. On rivers with a low general stock of fish, and the otter's favourite food of eels in serious decline, large barbel are especially vulnerable to otter predation, especially in cold winter conditions when they are inactive.

Habitat

To thrive, barbel need clean, well oxygenated water, plentiful food, and cover in the form of

It's dusk and the big barbel are feeding.

Using a tree to gain height or cover is helpful when barbel spotting in clear water.

weeds, reedbeds and overhanging bushes or other underwater features. Barbel have a preference for stony or gravel riverbeds rather than mud or silt. Anyone familiar with the Wye, middle Severn or Hampshire Avon or many similar rivers will have little difficulty in recognizing ideal barbel habitat.

Scientific studies have shown that where a river has been dredged or the cover and features removed, the barbel population slumps (along with that of other species), and where they can, the fish move to other, more favourable stretches. This destructive procedure removes the spawning areas, weeds and tree cover so vital to fish. Some anglers have recognized this and have worked to restore the river habitat, not just for barbel but fish generally. In Norfolk, much good work, led by Chris Turnbull among others, has been done and continues to be done

on the River Wensum. Similarly on the Yorkshire Swale, the River Swale Preservation Society is doing similar habitat restoration work that is paying off.

Feeding Habits

A further consideration concerning the barbel's feeding habits is that there are subtle differences from one river to another, partly due to its type – whether it is spate or chalk – or where it is located. Barbel in the northern part of the country, and most notably with fish from the Ribble, are more inclined to feed in lower temperatures. Ribble barbel are often caught in extreme winter conditions when barbel in more southerly rivers refuse to feed at all. Chub anglers on the Ribble are not surprised to hook into a barbel when fishing bread for chub when cat ice lines the river.

It is widely believed that barbel are mainly nocturnal feeders, but this is far from the truth. The fact that many of the biggest barbel are caught after dark is more a testament to the fact that many big barbel *anglers* fish at that time, the myth being perpetuated by would-be big barbel anglers reading the reports of the captures of these big fish being caught in the dark hours and then emulating the captors. Barbel anglers of wide experience know full well that barbel can be caught at any time when the conditions are right – although they do recognize that very often the conditions are at their best when darkness falls. The 'secret' is not to be a slave to fishing at any particular period in the twenty-four hours of the day, but to be alert to the conditions and to fish accordingly, whenever they are at their best. Of course, anglers who work regular hours through the day and who wish to fish between weekends have no choice but to fish in the evening and a few hours into darkness. This fact also goes a long way to perpetuating the myth that barbel are mainly nocturnal feeders.

It is true, however, that barbel often have one of their active periods in a twenty-four-hour cycle from around dusk, or shortly after dusk, which on many rivers lasts for no more than a couple of hours or so; the next feeding period usually follows well after midnight, then with a dawn binge that can last until the sun comes up. Midday can be a very good feeding period on many rivers. On some very popular barbel stretches the fish come to expect food (bait) at certain busy barbel fishing times, and a feeding period is created where none might otherwise have come to exist had the fish been left to forage for nothing more than natural food. These feeding spells will, of course, vary in length and diversity according to the time of year, the water temperature, and the length of the daylight/darkness period, and will have to be considered in association with other environmental factors such as floods and dry spells, bright days and dull days, moonlit nights and dark nights, and so on – all of which factors tumble through an angler's mind when he processes his chances of catching fish to decide when, where and how.

It is also as well to remember that a shoal of barbel can be turned on at any time by judicious feeding, especially with particle baits such as maggots, casters, hemp and small pellets, and to some extent sweetcorn, where they have not become wary of it. Feed in enough particles at a steady but continuous rate, either by hand, catapult, baitdropper or swimfeeder and, given conditions that are some way towards being conducive to barbel feeding, barbel will respond. If you can maintain this feeding for at least twenty minutes without actually introducing a hookbait, barbel can be provoked into a state of uninhibited feeding. Don't be tempted to introduce a baited hook in the early stages, because you then run the risk of spooking the shoal with a hooked fish before they have reached that confident feeding frenzy where the fish are competing with each other for the bait and in so doing have lost, or are ignoring, most of their natural wariness. There is no doubt that when this feeding method works it can be the basis for some tremendous barbel catches.

It is a method that is much more likely to work on stretches of river that are heavily stocked with 'shoal' barbel – that is, where the barbel are around 3–7lb or so and in shoals of around a dozen or more strong. And if there are shoals of chub present, then the competitive element will come into play with these fish, too. In clear water and from an elevated position such as a high bank or a tree, you can see the competitive element at work, with the smaller barbel and chub vying for the bait, the smallest fish grabbing at the food while it is still sinking and the larger fish often holding station at the rear of the shoal, waiting for the 'safe' titbits to escape the shoal.

Fishing for solitary, or near solitary, big barbel requires an entirely different method, because there are usually not enough fish of any species for you to explore the competitive element. Stalking and discretely introducing just a little loose feed, or even a single hookbait, stationary or rolled, is more the order of the day. Lots of loose feed will only serve to overfeed a solitary fish, and may even cause it to slink off to a nearby bolt hole in the weed and remain there until it feels safe.

2 THE APPROACH TO CATCHING BARBEL

That old adage 'first find your fish' applies as much to barbel as any other fish. It has been said a thousand times before but cannot be repeated often enough: you cannot catch fish that are not there, and even the best methods and the best baits are all totally redundant in empty swims. Locating barbel is therefore always first on the catching agenda, and the first task of all is to determine which river you will be fishing for barbel – not a daunting task these days, as most rivers in the UK now have barbel.

Finding a Water

The type of river that you fish for barbel is partly dictated by where you live, to a great extent by how far you are prepared to travel, and if you wish to fish for just any barbel, or for that special, headline-grabbing whopper. How far you travel can be on the basis of a single day or for longer trips, such as taking a holiday in another part of the country. It may be that over the course of the year you will get to fish a number of different rivers with very different characteristics and which need different approaches. Or maybe you are one of those lucky individuals with a wide variety of barbel waters within a reasonable distance of your home, and can vary your approach from fun fishing for shoal fish on prolific barbel stretches, to the stealthy hunt for the big one on an exclusive club water.

The waters you fish are also dictated by the access you can obtain. This could be day ticket, weekly or season ticket, through club membership or syndicate membership, although there are few river syndicates to choose from. The cost of all this access can soon add up to a tidy sum, further tempered by whether you can actually gain membership in the case of clubs or

syndicates with much sought-after waters and with waiting lists to match.

Other factors can play a part. Is the access suited to your physical ability? Does it involve long walks over rough terrain, or have difficult or dangerous banks? Is it the sort of water that you will enjoy fishing? Is it often crowded and heavily fished with a constant rush to claim a good swim? The factors that are important to you should be considered as they will all have some impact on your fishing enjoyment.

Your approach to finding venues depends on several factors, the most important being whether there is barbel fishing close to where you live. If it's within an hour's drive, then finding out what and where should be straightforward. But if you need to travel further afield, which is still true for many areas despite the continuing spread of barbel, then you will need to plan your chosen venue with more care. It is certainly much easier to get to know a barbel water if it's close to home.

It may be that you don't mind travelling, or can afford both the time and cost of doing so, or that you're prepared to make your barbel fishing part of a trip away from home for some other reason, in which case distance may be no object. Wherever the potential venue, you'll need to do some research. Local tackle shops are one starting point and worth a try. Studying Ordnance Survey maps and taking a look is another, though somewhat restricted if the venue is on private land. However, many rivers have a public footpath running close to or actually along the riverbank, and you may spot the controlling club's 'Private fishing' notices on bankside trees and fences, often with a contact phone number.

Angling guide books and pamphlets also list waters and clubs in the area. At least a couple of areas of the Environment Agency produce these

A permit such as this Ringwood DAA one has plenty of barbel fishing available – in this case the famous Throop Fishery.

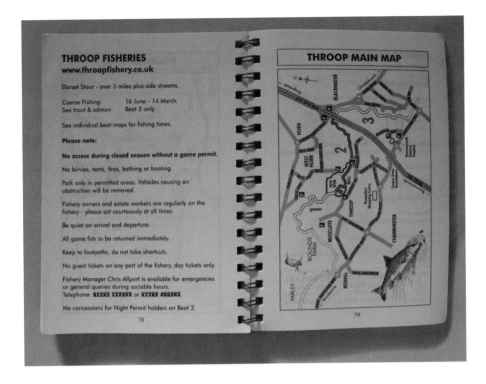

guides at very modest cost (the one for the South West is especially good), and they are a good starting point in finding out about day ticket and club waters, with details of cost and contact details. There may also be angling magazine and newspaper features from time to time that describe popular or potential barbel waters.

Finally, many fisheries and angling clubs have their own websites that will have all the information that you require.

River Types

River fishing (on some rivers, at least) is perhaps the last bastion of pioneering angling where it is still possible to find one or two almost wild and deserted stretches holding fish that have never been caught. Certainly this applies to some parts of the River Dove in Derbyshire and some Yorkshire rivers. Less than ten years ago Graham spent two years fishing a few miles of the Dove where there were no signs of other anglers, and where in many areas he had to cut his way through the undergrowth to find the

river. Although he didn't catch anything special in the way of barbel he treasures the experience, as the fishing was among the wildest and most adventurous he has ever enjoyed, providing a feeling of exploration that must be quite unique among modern anglers.

Big Spate Rivers

Perhaps the most challenging river type is the big spate river. It is likely to have a rocky or

This overgrown stretch of the Dorset Stour holds barbel, but it is almost a mile from the nearest access point.

The flooded Cheshire Dane in winter, but even in summer it can rise rapidly.

stony bottom with gravel in places. There may be huge boulders or rocky gulleys to contend with, and above all it is likely to be prone to sudden spates when heavy downpours flash flood the river. Being rain-fed it is liable to be cooler than a spring-fed chalk stream, as well as more acidic.

With powerful flows and a changing and snaggy riverscape, this type of river is tough on tackle, and needs a positive approach to get the best out of it. You need to be able to feed and fish accurately at long distance, as well as hold bottom in strong flows. Big rivers can take a lot of bait, too, especially when it's being washed away quickly. Playing barbel in these conditions needs careful thought beforehand. Your gear is tested by the current as well as by the barbell, with the additional wear and tear from rocks and other snags.

Typical big spate rivers include the Wye, Severn, Swale, Ribble and Trent, and it is clear that even within this category there is considerable variation. But all these rivers and others besides represent some challenging barbel fishing. Perhaps their best aspect is the amount of river available, which means lots of barbel and

The Wye is a magnificent river; it is prone to spates, but holds plenty of good barbel.

The Kennet, seen here in winter, has long been renowned for its barbel.

This bend on Throop Fisheries on the Dorset Stour was so renowned it was named 'Barbel Corner', and despite changes to the riverbed there are still barbel nearby.

miles of riverbank, with a number of stretches isolated from the crowds, including anglers or anyone else.

As well as being prone to fast flooding, with levels increasing by several feet or more following a few days of heavy rain, spate rivers – unlike the clear chalk streams – turn to the colour of chocolate, heavy with sediment, which very often is the trigger for the barbel to feed with abandon. Densely coloured water makes it easier for you to approach and fish right in the margins where the slacker water can usually be found.

Chalk Streams

A number of chalk streams hold barbel in England; these include the Hampshire Avon, Kennet, Windrush and Lea. Fed by springs on the chalk downland, these alkaline rivers have a mostly gravel bottom and are rich in natural food and weed. Their clear water, low banks and generally constant flow make for challenging fishing as well as delightful surroundings. Although their flow is mostly constant, at some point during the early winter it is increased when the winterbournes start flowing, and this extra flow will usually last right through until the following June.

No matter how much chalk streams flood, they always retain a great degree of clarity compared to spate rivers, and whereas spate rivers reach a point following a heavy flood where the water is so infused with sediment that it deters fish from feeding, this rarely happens on the chalk streams.

Clay Vale Rivers

Clay vale rivers include the Great Ouse, Dorset Stour and Thames. Due to the varied geology of their catchment areas, they do not fit easily into the first two categories. Take, for example, the Dorset Stour: the upper river above Blandford is clay vale, and when it rains it is quick to flood and colour up; yet below Blandford, several small chalk streams join the river, and these tend to run clear. Many group the Stour with the nearby Hampshire Avon, but the variance in flow rates, especially in summer, demonstrates at least part of the difference between them. Thus the Stour generally has a very low flow rate in late summer and early autumn, whereas the nearby Avon maintains its spring-fed flows much more consistently. The Stour stretches that hold barbel below Wimborne do bear some resemblance to the Avon, however, with plenty of weed and gravel.

Other Rivers

Navigable rivers such as the Thames are an altogether different proposition. Fed by a mixture of

limestone streams, chalk streams and clay vale rivers, the main River Thames is much disturbed by boat traffic in the summer months. The pounded lengths are sluggish in summer, with little weed surviving the discoloration caused by the boats, and barbel location is difficult. Yet there are parts of the Thames where there is no boat traffic and which are hospitable to barbel, such as the weir pools and some side streams.

Small Rivers

Small rivers present a different set of problems: they may be no more than a miniaturized version of one of the above, part of the upper reaches of a larger river, or a side stream or perhaps just a small river. This type of river is

LEFT: *Wolvercote: Oxford angling legend, the late Peter Stone, once observed barbel ascending this weir on a Thames side-stream. Today, a plaque on the bridge commemorates his angling achievements.*

BELOW: *A big barbel such as this one of 13lb 6oz caught by Gary Knowles is a cracking fish and big enough to make any angler smile.*

often only ten yards wide, perhaps even less. When fishing, you could be very close to the barbel at all times, which means that a stealthy approach is vital. On small, clear streams, although it is more of a problem keeping out of sight of the fish, it is usually much easier to spot them. Often some of the biggest barbel come from the smallest streams.

Approaches to Barbel Fishing

What do you want from your barbel fishing? There is a great variety of approaches, and for many keen anglers, barbel fishing is just one facet of the numerous and varied types of fishing for the diverse species they tackle in the course of a year. When conditions are right for the species they'll put the bulk of their time in seeking barbel, knowing that being circumspect in their choice of fishing according to conditions they will most likely be successful. Picking the right time – as often as not late summer and through autumn where barbel are concerned – they'll enjoy it all the more for knowing their chances of catching barbel are at their best.

An increasing number of anglers, however, just want to catch barbel, any barbel, and have little or no interest in any other species. They have come to appreciate barbel for their magnificent fighting qualities, and the fact that chasing them puts them on the banks of some great-looking rivers. The size of the barbel they catch isn't particularly important to them, but the thrill of hunting and catching them is. Of course, the occasional big one puts the icing on an already tasty cake, but consistently catching any size of barbel is what turns them on.

For others, hunting the biggest barbel is the only way to go, with the necessary more patient approach both acknowledged and accepted. The specimen barbel hunter seeks out the rivers that hold the biggest fish, and then makes it his business to discover the particular stretches and the swims where they are usually found. He will fish all through the night, covering the dusk and dawn periods to be sure he is there at the optimum times, and will often rove for miles in search of the biggest fish.

An artificial caster is more durable than the real thing and better able to withstand the attentions of tiddlers.

The 'Open' Approach

Many anglers prefer to fish in an 'open' kind of way that doesn't particularly target either big or small barbel and is open to catching other species, such as chub, as well. This works well where there is a big head of chub with the occasional barbel, and the barbel are of a similar or slightly larger size than the chub. This means that you can confidently tackle the chub knowing that your gear is sufficiently robust to handle any barbel that turn up.

Two approaches for this type of fishing spring to mind: the main one is a simple swimfeeder set-up using plenty of hemp and casters, both proven attractors for chub and barbel. The idea is to build up the swim and catch whatever invades it first, which is usually the chub. At worst, you'll have a good day's chub fishing, and if all goes to plan you'll get a few barbel, too.

The second approach is to float fish, again using plenty of hemp and caster as feed. During your session, if you become aware that barbel have moved into the swim, you may need to change tactics to fish harder on the bottom, but mostly you can keep to the same tactics. Occasionally, when both chub and barbel have moved on to the bait, the chub tend to rise from the bottom to intercept the bait while the barbel remain on or close to the bottom to feed there. By shotting the float to get the bait down to the bottom quickly you can go some way towards avoiding the chub and selecting the barbel.

This approach is best suited to fishing with what is the modern version of 'Avon' gear: a medium swimfeeder rod or Avon rod for the leger tactics, coupled with 6–8lb line, or a 'power' float rod with 6lb line for float fishing. In both cases it is essential to have carefully balanced tackle, and to fish open, snag-free water. Where this approach falls down is where the barbel are of a much bigger average size or you are likely to encounter barbel over about 7–8lb, or where there is a lack of other fish of comparable size. Chub are not the only other fish that may respond to this approach: on some waters you will encounter sizeable bream, too.

Whether this approach is worthwhile depends very much on the waters you are fishing, but finding sizeable chub sharing waters with barbel is commonplace, and being able to catch both barbel and chub from the same swim with the same tactics should make for more consistent sport. Bear in mind, however, that in many waters the barbel have grown much bigger than even ten years ago, and that the tackle that is suited to even big chub may be under-gunned for big barbel. This approach was highly successful on the middle reaches of the Hampshire Avon in the late 1990s when Mark had many excellent catches of big chub that often included one or more barbel. Mostly, Mark took these catches using feeder tactics but some swims were suited to float tactics, and the bait combination was always hemp and casters.

There is a big disadvantage to this approach, in that by catching plenty of chub and other fish there is a possibility that the activity will scare the barbel away unless you can get them competing with the chub and other fish. When this happens, the barbel often bully the other fish out of the swim. You may sense this happening when the swim where you were regularly pulling chub out, suddenly goes quiet; the next thing you know the rod is hooped over and a barbel is heading downstream like a train.

Catching Bags of Barbel
Perhaps the natural progression from the open approach is on venues that have a big head of shoal barbel. The tackle and tactics are not

especially different from the open approach, but the result is likely to be much more barbel focused. The size of the barbel will dictate the tackle required, as will the type of water.

Where it does differ from the open approach is that finding the barbel shoals is now an essential element, and rather than just hoping that the barbel will appear whilst we fish openly for anything that chances to come along, we are now sharply focused on our target species. Even on prolific stretches, the barbel are more often than not concentrated into certain areas and swims, and there will be hotspots. This approach demands knowledge of where those swims are, and how and when to tackle them.

The Static Approach to Catching Big Barbel
Three decades and more ago the open approach and the barbel-bagging approach were the norm for most anglers – but this was when barbel were still becoming established on many rivers that had not long been stocked, and were still growing and finding their niche in their new environment. Like any new species to a fishery, there will be several years when they breed prolifically and large shoals roam the river. As they become established they settle down to better fit their new home, the shoals become smaller and the average size increases. On some rivers, or some particular stretches of river, the fish rarely spawn successfully, and the few barbel that remain grow fat on the food that they no longer have to share with so many others. Another factor is that the barbel that were stocked in the middle reaches of a river gradually infiltrate the upper and lower reaches, some of them growing to a much greater size in their new home.

Consequently, on many barbel waters the emphasis has changed from being able to catch plenty of shoal barbel to having to find the few large barbel remaining, or those few barbel that made it to the upper and lower reaches. Many of these fish are in double figures, and some of them likely to have been caught many times before. In any event, they are going to be wary fish that have either seen it all before, or have seen very little of the bait that barbel anglers use and therefore need some educating. This means

On big rivers such as the Wye a static 'bait and wait' approach is most likely to pay dividends.

that your tactics must be exactly right to have any chance of catching them. The conditions will also play a greater part, in that much of the time the barbel may not be particularly interested in feeding, or at least only cautiously. Getting to know your chosen venue intimately is very wise.

Big barbel may be creatures of habit, but that doesn't mean that they will always be found in the same swims. Indeed, big barbel have been known to travel a mile or more in a day: one particularly famous big fish that held the barbel record on a few occasions was named 'The Traveller' due to its habit of being caught in several different swims throughout the 1½ mile stretch of the upper Great Ouse that contained it. Big barbel can be very cautious when feeding in some areas, yet prove vulnerable when ambushed on their route between swims. This is down to them instinctively associating danger with swims from where they have been caught on numerous previous occasions. That said, it doesn't mean that they cannot be caught in their regular haunts, only that you may have to put considerably more effort into fooling them through careful and precise feeding and bait presentation. You may find that they are only willing to take a bait if it is presented under the

cover of a tree raft or directly beside a weedbed, rather than in open water.

You also need to gear your tackle to big barbel: there is no room for compromise as was the case in either of the less specialized barbel approaches where you might get away with typical big chub gear using a medium feeder or Avon rod. From the rod downwards you need the right gear to get the better of big, hard-fighting fish that probably live in or very close to some kind of snag. For fish of this size, the float-fishing approach is rarely practical. Float fishing with 6lb line is all right for shoal barbel in open water, but big ones really need 8lb line as a minimum, fished well away from snaggy areas – and even then float fishing with such a relatively heavy line becomes clumsy when trotting the bait through the swim. Legering has two advantages; first, it allows the use of a heavier line and a heavier rod; and second, it enables you to fish patiently for many hours without the disturbance and effort that comes with continual trotting.

Fishing for big barbel requires confidence, and you will need patience and perseverance, too. It won't be easy, for the simple reason that big barbel, like most big fish of any species, are not found in abundance. At best a big barbel will be part of a very small group, and the biggest barbel with often be individual fish that rarely remain in a small area of the river. The toughest part can be not knowing why you're failing when you're going through a series of blank sessions. Is it because you haven't found the big fish, or are you doing something wrong? Is it time for a change of method, a change of bait, or even a complete change of location? The doubts creep in. Nevertheless, the wisest anglers realize that everyone goes through a bad patch every so often, and that it will go away as suddenly as it arrives. Very often a bad run is followed by a purple patch. Fishing for big barbel, like fishing for any outsize specimen fish, is a case of swings and roundabouts, and you learn that you have to go along with whatever fate offers.

Yet regardless of the inevitability of blank spells, you have to keep striving for an answer: after all, that is what fishing for big fish is about – not accepting that there is nothing you can do. Now and again you have to stop and take stock, go back to the basics and work your way along the accepted route that sooner or later leads to a

big fish: locate the fish; decide how to tackle the location, when to fish, which rig, which bait, and how to feed it – should we feed it, or go for the single hookbait and no feed approach?. Is there room to fish two rods, giving us the chance to fish two different areas of the swim, perhaps with two different baits? Will we be fishing open water and can therefore fish a little lighter than normal, or are we close to snags, meaning we have to fish heavier? These are questions you'll need to find the answers to. It is better to spend more time in planning and preparation than to settle yourself down in the first likely swim you come across, chuck some bait in and rig up your usual rig and start fishing. That's the good thing about blank sessions; they make you think, and very often they lead to you coming up with a better method, a better rig or a better bait. Best of all, digging your way out of a run of blanks leads to you being a better angler all round.

Moving Baits for Barbel

Some rivers with an ample head of barbel and where the banks are not overpopulated with

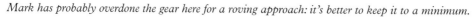

Mark has probably overdone the gear here for a roving approach: it's better to keep it to a minimum.

anglers respond well to a roving approach, using a bait that trundles and rolls its way through the swims. Float fishing could do this well were it not for the necessity of such heavy gear. The next best option is to leger the bait in such a way that the leger weight is not so heavy it will hold the bait static. The amount of weight you use is critical, it needs to be heavy enough to get the bait down to the bottom and allow it to trundle through the swim at the same pace as the current. Too heavy and it will not move enough, too light and it will roll away too quickly. If anything it is best to err on the slightly heavier side, for static baits will catch barbel but baits that move faster than the current rarely do. A slightly heavier weight can be encouraged to move with subtle flicks of the rod tip.

There are several crucial aspects to this type of fishing. The first one is finding a suitable venue. It is essentially a short range method and relies on being able to get close to the fish without spooking them. It is vital that you give other anglers plenty of space; it's not unknown for beginners at this method to trundle their baits through others' swims, which is a definite method of antagonizing them. Keeping in touch with your bait at all times is important, too, to detect bites and to present it in a natural way.

The Quick Hit Approach

Anglers with plenty of energy and a lack of patience can try the quick-hit approach to catching barbel, which can be especially productive on those stretches you know well. The idea is to travel light: one made-up leger rod, a landing net, and a bag of your favourite hookbaits. The idea is to visit several of the known barbel swims along the stretch. You quietly move into a swim, feed a little bait (or none at all if you deem it wise not to in a particular swim), introduce your hookbait as discreetly as possible, and then give the barbel ten to fifteen minutes to respond. If no bites or signs of fish are forthcoming you move to the next swim and do exactly the same thing. You can then repeat the whole procedure in each swim on the way back to where you started.

Carbelling

Carbelling is a play on words – part carp fishing,

Sunset on the lower Trent and the barbel are falling to a carbelling approach. (Courtesy of Bob Roberts)

part barbel fishing. It is an approach to barbel fishing that is borrowed heavily from the carp angler's approach in that it involves at least two heavy rods geared up with heavy tackle, which probably sit on a rod-pod fitted with bite alarms. Furthermore, the carper's standard static approach of bivvying up and fishing for two or more nights is also pursued. It isn't a style that is loved by some barbel anglers, but there is no doubt that it is a style that produces some of the best results on the big rivers such as the tidal Trent and the lower Severn.

All the approaches mentioned in this chapter will be discussed in much greater depth in Chapter 8 'Standard Rigs and Methods' and Chapter 9 'Other Rigs and Methods'.

3 BARBEL WATERS AND FINDING PRODUCTIVE SWIMS

Factors in Barbel Distribution

River Zones

Knowing that barbel live in your chosen river is one thing; finding them is another. The numerous rivers that hold barbel in the UK don't necessarily hold them from their narrowest upper reaches to the sea; for a variety of reasons, as discussed in this chapter, it is often the case that certain stretches are much better for barbel than others. This is because, in a river's course from tiny brook to wide, slow tidal estuary, some stretches are much more suited to the type of environment that best suits the barbel's requirements, not only for it to survive but also to thrive. The section of river that has the required flow, enough weed and other cover, and is reasonably clean and pollution free, is likely to be the barbel zone – the zoning system is used by biologists to define the areas throughout the length of a river.

Upstream of the barbel zone is the grayling zone; further upstream still is the trout zone. Downstream of the barbel zone is the bream zone. In each case there will be some overlap – we can expect to find other species apart from the one that lends its name to the zone. In the barbel zone, we will find at least traces of chub, dace, perhaps roach and even bream.

Few rivers, of course, comply perfectly with the zoning model. Some lowland rivers such as the Test and Itchen are almost entirely trout zone, whereas a river such as the Nene is the opposite, being mostly bream zone. In both cases barbel are adaptable enough to live in these rivers. But at least it does give us a starting point on finding barbel; in slow rivers we look for faster stretches or those near weirs, in very fast rivers we look for steadier stretches, and in those ideal rivers such as the Wye and Severn we will find barbel in many stretches.

The Hampshire Avon with 'streamer weed' (ranunculus) in full flower – barbel country.

TOP RIGHT: Old Iford Bridge, the site of Victorian barbel transfers to the Dorset Stour.

BOTTOM RIGHT: The Environment Agency and the Barbel Society are jointly developing a barbel replenishment programme. Here, Pete Reading assists a stocking exercise on the Dorset Stour. (Courtesy of Pete Reading)

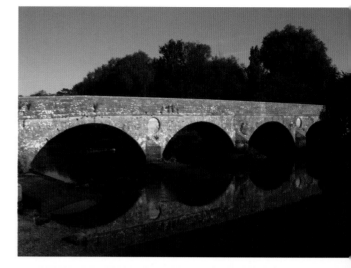

Pollution and Other Barriers

One limiting factor to finding barbel may be pollution. Many rivers that are otherwise well suited to barbel have been polluted for many decades. In recent years, the clean-up of these rivers in industrial areas has continued, although occasional pollutions may hinder progress. The upper Trent, together with its major tributary the Tame, was too polluted to hold any fish not that many years ago, but the clean-up continues such that at the time of writing (2010) barbel are now well established in both rivers, upstream almost as far as Stoke-on-Trent on the River Trent. And of course barbel thrive in that other tributary of the Trent, the Dove. Similarly, some Lancashire, Cheshire and Yorkshire rivers have been cleaned up to the extent that they hold fish for the first time in many years, and barbel are becoming established in them. This process takes time, however, and there may be setbacks from periodic pollutions.

Likewise the barbel's ability to populate a length of river may be hindered by weirs and other structures. On the Dorset Stour, for example, the original stocking more than a hundred years ago took place at Iford Bridge, the head of the tidal reaches. The barbel could spread upstream without hindrance as far as Throop Mill, which is less than four miles upstream (the situation has changed in more recent years with the construction of several weirs), and it was mainly because of restocking and fish being transferred upstream that barbel are found much further upstream today. In the early 1970s, a number of anglers transferred barbel (illegally) to Wimborne. In the 1990s, the EA stocked several stretches including Hampreston and Stourpaine, and much more recently, several stretches between Blandford and Wimborne. These stockings have enabled the spread of barbel that the numerous weirs would otherwise have prevented naturally.

Stocking

One factor in barbel distribution is whether barbel have been stocked in a water, how successful that stocking was, and how long they have been present. Over the past 120 years there have been many stockings of barbel: they may have been introduced into new waters, or have reinforced existing stocks, and this process has accelerated in recent years due to the popularity of barbel as a quarry for anglers and the willingness of the EA to supply young barbel from its huge fish farm at Calverton.

Simply stocking barbel into a new water, no matter how suitable, is no guarantee of success in the longer term. The long-term survival of barbel in a river depends on the fish's ability to reproduce and maintain its population. On some rivers, the Severn, Trent and Wye being especially good examples, barbel have proliferated and spread. Not only are these two rivers well suited to barbel, they have ideal conditions for spawning.

Contrast this to the upper Thames and its tributaries above Oxford, where the removal of spawning gravels through navigational dredging, combined with excessive predation by otters, has made the barbel's hold in the river tenuous. In the long term, the re-establishment of spawning areas and restocking may rectify the situation.

Other rivers lie somewhere between these two extremes as far as maintaining their barbel population is concerned.

Predation

The re-establishment of otters on many British rivers is having a definite impact on the barbel population in some areas. In winter, when barbel are generally less active, the otters have little difficulty in catching and killing them, and on waters with only a small number of barbel this can quickly lead to the decimation of the population. It is too early to know what the long-term effects of this additional predation will be; it is possible that some rivers will struggle to maintain their barbel populations without being regularly restocked with small barbel, and their potential to hold very big barbel will be limited.

Locating Barbel Swims

Barbel, like most fish, will seek to live where it best suits them in a river. The essentials that they seek naturally are a food supply, well oxygenated water, cover, and a flow in which they feel most comfortable most of the time in variable conditions. Favourite spots can include undercut banks, underneath the thick tresses of ranunculus (water crowfoot) beds, behind underwater boulders, and weirpools, and areas

Big barbel such as this one have proved vulnerable to otter predation on a number of rivers.

where they can find rest and sanctuary when heavy floodwater makes most of the river a raging torrent.

Before you start exploring stretches of river ensure that you have permission to be on the bank (club membership, or prior permission from the fishery owner or bailiff, unless there's a public footpath) and carry the proof! There is nothing more embarrassing than meeting the bailiff and being unable to justify why you are on the banks of a private stretch of river. It's no use claiming that you intend buying a ticket or permit. Furthermore, even if you are a club member, check your permit: you may find there is no access during the close season or when game fishing is taking place. If you do meet the bailiff, then be polite and explain what you are doing; it's surprising how well many bailiffs know their water, and with the right attitude towards them, most will give you pointers to where barbel can be found.

Another part of the preparation before you go exploring stretches of potential barbel river is to ensure you have polarized sunglasses, some sort of peaked hat, and are wearing drab clothing. There's no great necessity to wear full camouflage clothing – but since such clothing is now a fashionable part of the best dressed angler's attire, why not? And a good pair of stout, waterproof walking boots will make covering several miles of river a much more comfortable experience.

Study the club permit maps, Ordnance Survey maps or even Google Earth to get a feel for boundaries, and features such as bends, weirs and side streams. You may want to carry a notepad and pencil to make notes and sketches of likely swims, and a digital camera or mobile phone with built-in camera to take shots of potential swims.

Barbel Swims on Popular Waters

On many popular stretches of river that hold barbel, finding the best barbel swims is not very difficult. A quiet walk along the bank at the height of summer on a weekend should leave you in no doubt as to the likely swims, because the barbel anglers and their unmistakable tackle will be well in evidence. Depending on the water and the conditions, it may even be possible to

A lightweight rod quiver makes travelling light a simple job.

spot barbel. Provided you keep well back from where other anglers are fishing so as not to 'skyline' them (the sudden appearance of your silhouette on the skyline), and tread softly, you can learn much from this type of reconnaissance. You may be able to ask the anglers whether they've had any success without unduly disturbing them, though it is probably best to give them all plenty of room by keeping well back from the water's edge for at least fifty yards both up and downstream of their fishing position. The more you show respect for their right to fish undisturbed, the more likely they will be to offer helpful information.

If it's possible to see the type of swim that anglers appear to be fishing for barbel without disturbing either the angler or the fish, try to spot the obvious features in the swim. Note how the river is flowing, the position of weedbeds and other snags. Look for changes in depth, and evidence of the type of bottom such as gravel or rock. Pay particular attention to the patterns that the current forms at the surface, especially where a pronounced flow meets a slacker area

John Searl, keeping still and using the cover of reeds, tries to spot barbel in the gin-clear waters of the Hampshire Avon.

and forms a crease. If you can't get close enough at the time, make a point of returning to the swim at another time when no one is fishing it and then you can explore it thoroughly, including plumbing the depths at different spots.

As you explore further afield on the same stretch, see if you can spot similar swims, especially those that are far from the car park. There is an expression about this, known as the 'three field rule': all it means is that very few anglers ever get as far as three fields away from the car park, which is about half a mile on most waters. If you're prepared to travel light when you fish you can turn this to your advantage, even on heavily fished waters, unless they are very short stretches or have many access points.

Fish Spotting in Clear Rivers
One of the best times to look at a new stretch is high summer when the water is low and crystal clear. When the sun is high it is much easier to see deep into the water and spot the underwater contours, weedbeds, snags and, with the right approach, some barbel. Whenever possible try to walk upstream, as it is less likely that the fish will spot you. Although they view the terrestrial world through a 'window' above their heads, there will be many feeding fish tilted, even only slightly, towards the riverbed and so their 'window' will be angled upstream. In these clear conditions it will pay to stop for at least fifteen

minutes in likely spots. Your approach along the bank needs to be stealthy – it's no good scaring everything for fifty yards in front of you as you walk along the bank. Keep still and don't move your feet, and if possible make use of bankside cover so that you are not skylined.

Once in position, it's a case of patience and observation. Barbel can be hard to spot even in clear water; the giveaways are usually the coral pink pectoral fins and the darker shadow they cast over the lighter gravel, so well do they blend in. Another giveaway is the flash of white belly as they rapidly flip belly to surface in the current: the theory behind this strange behaviour is that they are intercepting food in midwater. The skill of fish spotting, and particularly barbel, is something that can't be learnt overnight but has to be developed over a period of time; the more you practise and develop those skills, the more often you will spot barbel when other anglers walk past them and remain unaware of their presence.

Big Rivers and Reading the Surface
On much bigger rivers such as the Severn, Wye, Ribble and Trent, it is improbable and often impossible to spot barbel in the same way that you can in much smaller and possibly clearer rivers. What you can do though is read the river by noting the speed of the current and learning how to interpret the various patterns and nuances that form on the surface. Each of those patterns denotes a change in current, which is usually a manifestation of the current having to flow through or around some feature on the river bed. The geography of the bottom may include boulders and other solid snags, and these cause a greater surface disturbance than such as a weedbed, where the water can flow through. In places, the current will steady as the water deepens, or quicken as it shallows.

Generally speaking, the amount of turbulence at the surface is the sum of the speed of the current and the size of the obstruction on the riverbed. Most often, areas where the water boils at the surface are best avoided. However, a relatively small, distinctly turbulent area contained within a smooth glide usually means the water is flowing over a single larger than normal boulder or possibly a snagged tree branch that is

Even the upper Trent is a big river in some parts and needs specialized tackle and tactics to catch the barbel.

lying on an otherwise level and reasonably smooth riverbed. Behind such a disturbance will be a calmer patch of water, and these patches are especially attractive to barbel, for they offer respite from the current and a trap where food will collect in the lee of the snag where the bottom has been scooped out somewhat by the diverted current.

A bend in the river will send the main current to the outside of the bend where the water is faster and where the current on the inside of the bend is considerably slower, possibly even slack in places. Very often there are areas where the faster water butts up to the slower water and forms what is popularly known as a crease, which often denotes a notable swim. But more about that later. With experience, you will be able to recognize the subtle differences between the surface swells caused by submerged rushes, the ripples caused by streamer weed, and those caused by shallow water over various grades of gravel or silt.

Bear in mind that being able to read the surface is by no means an advantage solely on big rivers, for even a small stream will not always run clear and very often the surface will be battered by wind and rain making seeing though the surface a near impossibility.

Another feature of parts of the Severn and Trent, and to a much lesser extent the Wye, is the use of permanent pegs. These permanent concrete stakes, in place as numbered swim markers for angling competitions, give a point of reference on many stretches that are otherwise featureless. By asking around you should be able to determine likely barbel swims. You may find match anglers less secretive in this regard than those who specialize in catching barbel. If you add your ability to get to 'read' the river with knowledge gained from collating catch reports, a pattern may emerge. You may spot the pattern that signifies that a certain type of swim holds barbel.

Remember that on a big river simply fishing the right peg is far from the whole story; on a river that could be up to a hundred yards wide you need to have a good idea where the barbel live. On some swims that could be close in, which is why it's worth noting the outside of bends where the main current is close in; often, however, this will be out in the middle of the main flow. So ask for more than just a peg number if you do find such information forthcoming. On stretches of river where there is little in the way of obvious features such as snags and weedbeds, and the riverbed is just rock, stone or gravel, look for slight depressions in the riverbed as these are natural holding spots for barbel.

Small Coloured Rivers

Some rivers such as the Teme, the Dove and the Dane are small in size yet run sufficiently coloured much of the time, making barbel spotting a fruitless pursuit. Yet being able to recognize the characteristics of a potential barbel

ABOVE: The Lugg is a typical small river with a reasonable head of barbel.

ABOVE: This small weir on the Cheshire Dane is just one of the many varied configurations of weir that may hold barbel. This one is renowned for them.

BELOW: Streamer weed on the Hampshire Avon; are barbel lurking underneath?

swim is vital, and as with the much bigger rivers, there are many visual clues to what is happening underwater. An advantage on these smaller rivers is that it is much easier to carefully plumb depths at close range to find drop-offs and depressions on the river bed.

Weirs and Mill Pools

There is no such thing as a typical weir or mill pool; these man-made structures may be modern and made of concrete, or centuries old and made of oak piles and stone. Their size varies from tiny gauging weirs to huge weir pools on major rivers such as the Trent or Severn, and no two weirs are the same. On pounded navigable rivers such as the Thames or Trent, weirs are part of the navigation, being adjacent to locks. What many weirs do possess, however, is an attraction to lovers of fast water such as barbel.

Weirs are always interesting to fish; some say that they rarely live up to their promise, but ignore them at your peril. The qualities that make them attractive to barbel include well oxygenated water, plenty of cover, the frequent presence of snags, and a strong chance of a good food supply. Ancient weirs often end up with underwater caverns right under the weir itself where the oak posts holding up the weir have rotted and the strong current has eroded the gravel behind them. Such a snaggy and 'safe' area suits barbel very well, and many anglers are unaware of its presence.

Weedbeds

Weedbeds are invariably barbel magnets. Barbel love to bury themselves in dense weed to forage for food, then glide out into the current to intercept food that is being swept downriver. And of course a weedbed can offer sanctuary from a strong current when a barbel needs to rest, and it offers cover and shade from a bright and hot sun. In short, weedbeds have a lot going for them, and a barbel angler will be wise to note where such weedbeds are when he roams the river when the water is low and clear and everything can be seen in much greater detail. Even in winter when the weed has died back, they can be excellent areas to fish as they will still harbour more natural food and provide a little

Graham checks out underwater snags during a closed season reconnaissance session.

more cover than the empty, more barren areas where no weed grows. The most common river weed is ranunculus, a long stranded weed that in some stretches of some rivers has all but taken over the riverbed; there are few rivers without any. Anglers tend to refer to it as streamer weed, as will this book.

Reeds and Rushes

Marginal reeds and rushes, and clumps that occasionally grow in mid-river, have all the same attractions as streamer weed and should be noted as potentially good barbel swims. An extra advantage of reeds and rushes where they grow in the margins is that they offer the angler some cover from the fish. Don't do as some anglers and beat down wide access holes to the river: try to fish through a natural gap, or make a gap just wide enough to poke a rod and play a fish.

Undercuts and Underwater Caverns

Some river banks, especially where a straight piece of fast water comes up against the outside of a bend, become eroded away and form deep undercuts, a few of them quite cavernous. This is especially the case where the bank has clumps of trees, because the roots strengthen the bank and prevent it collapsing. These can often be

good barbel swims, and good angling spots as long as the roots don't protrude too much into the water and become so snaggy they gobble up tackle and make landing a fish almost impossible should you manage to hook one. However, they are always worth a try – though do beware of the danger of the bank collapsing if you sit on top of the overhang. It is far safer, and better all round from a fishing point of view, if you sit several yards upstream of the undercut, cast as close to it as you can, and fish just heavy enough to allow the current to carry the baited tackle under the bank.

Swims in Changing Conditions

Always remember that as conditions change so does the nature of many swims, some becoming useless and others, which in different conditions were poor swims, turning into very attractive ones. Floodwater is the main cause of change, extra water creating some deeper, slacker areas along what were, in normal and low water conditions, very fast and shallow margins. Barbel are very much attracted to these temporarily slacker and more comfortable spots. (There is more about these swims and fishing floodwater in Chapter 10 'Seasonal Changes and Extreme Conditions'.)

Car Park Swims …

There is no doubt that prolific barbel waters with good access are often heavily fished, to the extent that many good swims are fished every day unless conditions are extreme, such as prolonged floods or gross snowmelt following a spell of heavy snowfall, when the barbel wouldn't feed anyway. On such a heavily fished water the barbel have seen it all before – and what is worse, having finally secured a hot swim, you have no way of knowing whether it has been grossly overfed the day before, or even the same day if you are snatching an evening session. The bottom line is that the popularity of the swims close to the car park is both to their advantage and their disadvantage.

Their disadvantage is that the barbel are wise and have learned that most of the baits used spell danger. However, they are often hungry enough to either ignore the danger, or try to avoid it while still taking baits – a stealthy approach and a good rig usually sorts them out. The advantage of car park swims is the sheer volume of bait that is being thrown in. Fish have two primary instincts: to procreate, and to feed – the one relevant to this discourse – and if they find an area where there is a rich and continual supply of easily obtained food they will not stray far from it, in spite of the obvious threat from anglers. Another advantage is that, due to the nature of most of the baits that barbel anglers use – namely very nutritious boilies and pellets – the barbel in that area will, at least to some extent, have an enhanced growth rate, giving the area extra potential for producing barbel with a high average size and a number of exceptionally large specimens.

… and Quiet Stretches

The advantage of swims that lie several fields – and a corresponding number of stiles or gates – away from the car park is that they will be rarely fished, at least in comparison to the car park swims. In theory, at least, the barbel in such areas will be less educated and more inclined to confidently take any baits that are offered. Another advantage is that you will have little or no problem finding a vacant swim and, most important to many anglers, the possibility, or at least the feeling, that you will find that rare dream fish, that monster barbel that has never graced a net before. For the most part it is a pipe dream, but it happens often enough to persuade many anglers that the long walk is worth the effort. And, of course, you often have a complete stretch to yourself to enjoy in quiet solitude.

It is surprising how many anglers are actually driven to take a long walk before fishing as they have it firmly planted in their minds that it is always the right thing to do. The reality,

This popular barbel swim on the Wye is just a short walk from the car park.

Walking Kit

If you're expecting to cover a few miles, proper walking boots are a must, although carrying a pair of waders in a rucksack for when you want to take a closer look at a swim is a wise move. For shorter walks you may be able to wear waders for the duration. It's also worth taking a long walking stick, a wading staff, or an extending landing-net handle (an alloy one may be better than a carbon-fibre one); this is useful in helping you keep your balance when wading in the faster swims and for probing the bottom, testing depths and so on. Wearing some sort of life jacket in dangerous areas when wading is also sensible. A pair of polarized glasses is essential for cutting out the reflections and getting the best views of the bottom, and of course fish spotting. Finally, take a bag or box of various baits that you can feed to any fish you spot to see how they react to it. This is best done in the last week or two leading up to your first session when the season opens. Other than that, all you need is some sensible clothing for walking, including waterproofs. Make up a flask and some sandwiches to go in your carryall if you're making a day of it, and maybe a waterproof cushion to sit on.

It can be worth taking a bucket of various baits when exploring during the closed season so that you can introduce a few free samples.

however, is that most of the big barbel caught are taken from car park swims which are well fed with highly nutritious food. So it boils down to a question of priorities: the odds in your favour of catching the biggest barbel; company rather than solitude; a short walk or a long one; and a possibility, however remote, of finding a monster barbel that was hitherto unknown. The choice is yours!

Using the Closed Season to Advantage

Many river anglers wield a paintbrush during the closed season, while others head for stillwaters to while away the time until they can get back on the rivers. But some make a least one trip to the river for a good recce, gathering information and preparing the way for 16 June. It's also a great excuse to take a very enjoyable walk along the river and soak up the atmosphere. It's surprising just how much atmosphere there is when you walk along a river at a time when you can't fish and all you can do is look and learn. It's as though your mind is a radio that has just tuned into a few extra stations that you didn't know were there because you were too busy listening to the old favourites. You find you're looking at the river in the same old way, with the ultimate aim of catching fish, but noticing things you've not paid so much attention to before, or taking notice of them in a different way – partly because you've got time as you're not itching to get a bait in, and also you're paying more attention to the river, and less to the fish.

Graham identifies a potential barbel-holding spot, in this case a slack behind a tree.

This 'special feeling' you get is a bonus, though: the other aspect of walking the river in the closed season is a purely practical learning experience.

Pick Your Time

If you can only make one sortie along your river, then choose your timing carefully. If the main purpose of your walk is to get an intimate picture of the swims, then the best time to do it is before the trees and vegetation are in full bloom, ideally not long after they've started to bud; then on the normally very overgrown stretches you won't have to fight your way to the water's edge to get a good look – at least not until you have earmarked a few spots for further visits, possibly with prebait (*see* Chapter 8 'Standard Rigs and Methods'), closer to opening day. This is another good time to take a close look at the swims when the weed and bankside cover have grown.

But no matter whether you choose to make early or late visits to the river, it is essential to do so when the water is clear and at least at its normal level, though low water levels are even

better. Remember, you are there to gather information, to take a good look at, and into swims, and possibly to spot fish. Coloured water is a bonus when the season opens and the priority is feeding fish.

Making Detailed Inspections

During the season, when you arrive at a river with tackle and bait, it's normal to take a walk to try and spot fish, bait a swim or two and plumb it before introducing a baited hook. This gives you a rough idea of the nature of the swim – but wouldn't it be good to already have a detailed picture in your mind's eye of the swim and surrounding area, and particularly the exact spot where your tackle is going to lie? During the season when you want to fish the same day, plumbing and prebaiting is as far as you can go because you need to make as little disturbance as possible: the last thing you want to do is spook the fish to the point that it will be hours before they return and feel confident enough to feed.

However, during close season explorations, it is possible to have a really good look. You can probe the swims with a stick, wade through them where they're shallow enough, and lift the weed to see what creatures it is harbouring and if there are any interesting depressions or other features. You can measure the depth to within an inch (at a given level), and get a really detailed picture of the contours of the bottom. Only one thing is better, and that is actually swimming beneath the surface and seeing what the fish see. Not many of us either want to or can do that, but if you can, then go for it, but stay safe.

Inspect those swims you already know, as well as new, untried swims: it's surprising how you can discover new hotspots in known swims once you know in detail what's down there. The winter floods may have changed the features of a known swim, too, so following a close season inspection you will be well prepared for the new season.

Shelves and Undercuts

As described earlier, where the current has undercut the bank the water gradually deepens from one bank to the other, generally, though not always, being at its deepest on the outside of bends.

Wade steadily across to a safe depth, taking note of weedbeds and clear gravel, and test the depth in detail, taking particular note of where the steepest drop-off is. If you can, go to the opposite bank and probe down into the undercut to test the depth and any snags that could cause problems.

Rafts of Floodwater Debris

Areas of floodwater debris are always interesting, but every time you fish one you don't really know (until you've had enough experience of fishing them) just what snags are waiting underneath. Many times we roll our baits beneath the raft and then find when we hook fish that we're actually pulling the fish into snags. There are plenty of little pitfalls like this that will catch us out until we know about them. So now's your chance to get your wading stick or extending landing net handle to have a thorough probe round. Some snags you may be able to remove – though be careful you don't get rid of those that are important to the fish, the ones that attracted them to that home in the first place.

Graham surveys the tail of a pool that might hold barbel.

Towards the Shallows

It's nice to lean on a convenient fallen tree, as in the picture, at a spot where the river bed rises. These are excellent areas for early summer fishing when the water has thoroughly warmed through. Food collects on the rise in the river bed, and if you keep still and out of sight, you can watch the fish gliding over the gravel between the weedbeds. You will soon note just which run they favour and work out how best to offer them a bait.

Deep Pools

There's not much you can do with the deeper pools as far as wading and probing are concerned, but it does no harm to keep low and simply watch for a while. You just never know what you're going to see when there is no lead or bait hitting the water to disturb the fish.

Flood Level Lines

As you walk along, take note of where the lines of flood debris are on the bank, and remember where the best looking spots were when the river was in flood. Now the water is low and clear, have a good look and a root around with your stick. Find any snags and estimate exactly where your bait will come to rest when the river is in flood. This is a very useful picture to have in mind when you next fish the swim when the level is up.

Gravel Bars

Yes, gravel bars do happen naturally in rivers, they're not just a product of excavated gravel pits! Make a note of these at low water and have a good look and a probe round the edges of them. These can be excellent swims when the level is up high enough to cover them.

Panoramic Views

On these close season walks, you may find yourself standing by a big bend in the river, or another spot that offers a good panoramic view upstream and downstream of the river. Just stand, stare, and do nothing more than observe. Think about all the creatures that live their lives in that piece of river. Look at the currents, the slacks, the fast water and the creases that divide the two. See the weed waving in the clear water, and occasionally watch the dark shapes of fish drifting in and out of them, clearly silhouetted as they glide over the clean gravel. It's good just to stand and stare sometimes, letting your mind drift as it tries to understand this other world.

It's good to walk, and even better to walk along a river at a time when you can do no more than look, learn and dream.

4 FEEDING AND BAITS

How Barbel Feed

Knowing how barbel feed can help us understand why certain baits are likely to be readily accepted by barbel; it also teaches us how to use these baits effectively as hookbaits, and how to use them to feed a swim.

The barbel's head shape gives several clues as to how it feeds. The underslung, tough mouth, the four barbules and the flat top to the head help the barbel use the water flow to keep it close to the bottom in a strong current, and are features which have evolved to suit its love of strong flowing water and the manner in which it feeds. The barbel is mainly a rooter, although it will take food from mid-water, and also has the curious ability – for a fish with an underslung mouth – to flip over and take food from the surface when it feels the need. Most often, however, it uses its barbuled snout to dig into riverbed gravel and silt, and can nudge aside large pebbles as much as six inches in diameter to seek out the food buried among the bottom debris. This aggressive feeding mannerism is quite unlike the relatively gentle picking of chub. Barbel detect the presence of food buried in the gravel through their taste buds dotted all round the mouth, and particularly on the barbules. They are quite capable of sniffing out and then rooting out a bait that is buried under two or three inches of silt or gravel.

Having nudged, prodded and generally disturbed the bed of the river, they then suck up the food that is revealed. The tough mouth enables them to 'graze' algae and other tiny forms of life clinging to stones. There is much natural food in the gravel, including snails, crayfish, stone loach, bullheads, stonefly larvae, caddis grubs, mayfly larvae, shrimps and the larvae of brook lampreys. In midsummer when the minnows are spawning barbel become temporarily predatory – although it does seem that barbel instinctively recognize 'fishy' or 'meaty' flavours, including some of the natural food already mentioned, such as small fish and, of course, worms. It is hardly surprising, therefore, that many successful barbel bait recipes include flavours resembling some kind of seafood, fish and various meats.

These tough, strong fish have yet another distinctive way of feeding: they will drop straight down on to a food item and engulf it with their mouth, with no sucking involved. This is just one of the reasons why the barbel is capable of giving such a savage bite, when the rod whips right round with hardly any warning at all: it has found the bait, dropped down on to it, mouthed it and turned downstream all in one movement. Because of this, apart from the hook being unmasked and free to do its job, there is no real

The barbel's barbules help it to 'taste' its food.

Any second now that rod tip's going to pull round …

advantage to hair-rigging – but more about this later.

It does seem that barbel instinctively recognize 'fishy' or 'meaty' flavours. These include some of the natural foods already mentioned, such as small fish and worms, and it is hardly surprising that many successful barbel bait concoctions use these flavours. The barbel has powerful pharyngeal teeth in its throat that enable it to crunch through hard pellets, fish, crayfish, caddis grub cases and snails with ease. This crunching sound is loud enough underwater to carry through the current and alert barbel (and chub, and others) to the fact that more fish are feeding, and attract them to the source. Underwater filming with audio quite clearly demonstrates this to be a fact.

Because barbel are a shoal fish, at least until their numbers are reduced and only a few solitary but very big fish remain, they tend to feed as a shoal, working upstream as they do so. There is an advantage to this, in that food items disturbed and missed by the leading fish of the shoal may be picked off by those behind. When the barbel at the head of the shoal reach the point where the feeding area peters out, they will often whip round, drop back and rejoin the shoal at the rear. It is as if the barbel are taking it in turns to feed, and it appears to be an instinctive behaviour. This sudden turning round to head back to the tail of the shoal is probably responsible for at least some of the tearaway bites typical of barbel.

When Barbel Feed

In the autumn, barbel tend to feed right though the day; in summer they may prefer to feed at dawn and dusk when light levels are low. They do feed at night, but may move into shallow water away from their daytime haunts. Patches of clean gravel are an indication of where barbel have cleaned the stones of algae during the night. Their feeding times do vary from one river to another, however, so always, initially at least, fish at different times of day and night for at least a season, in order to discover the optimum feeding times for barbel on your river. And even then, beware of falling into the trap of thinking that the barbel on your river feed mainly at night, say, because these usual patterns can and do change, and it pays to change your own fishing pattern occasionally to check that you're not missing out. Many times anglers have established the habit of fishing only at night, between the hours of dusk and dawn, and then found from a daylight fishing angler that he has consistently been catching more fish from the same swims. It may surprise some anglers to know that there are many rivers where the barbel feed best through the day rather than through the night, so never assume that night fishing is always best.

Weaning Barbel on to a Bait

It has long been known that if you throw enough bait into a barbel swim, sooner or later the barbel will recognize it as food and start feeding on it. This goes back to Victorian times when well-to-do anglers, with a paid assistant to do the donkey work, would fish swims on the Thames that had been baited with thousands of lobworms over the previous few days to get the barbel shoaled and accustomed to lobworm. Such a baiting pattern, where huge quantities of a particular bait have been introduced into a water, has been repeated, albeit unintentionally, many times on popular barbel venues. The Royalty Fishery on the Hampshire Avon at Christchurch has been the scene of several bait addictions (both by the barbel and the anglers!).

Early barbel pioneers fished lobworms, followed in turn by huge quantities of bread and bran groundbait. The use of vast amounts of Edam cheese was the next bait fixation,

The railway bridge on the Royalty Fishery where a succession of bait manias have dominated barbel fishing.

followed by the most controversial bait of all, maggots, thrown in by the gallon. Since then, and it was more than thirty years ago, many baits have succeeded on this venue, including luncheon meat, sweetcorn and the modern favourite, pellets and boilies. Nearby Throop Fishery on the Dorset Stour had so much hemp thrown in at the same time as the Royalty maggot craze that it was banned, both baits being banned due to the fear that the fish would become too preoccupied with a particular bait. Had maggots not become so expensive over the years, and pellets not so convenient, there is no doubt that maggot and caster fishing for barbel would have retained its appeal.

In each of these cases, the massive quantities of bait used weaned the barbel on to a specific bait. But often the converse is true. At the time of the Royalty maggot bonanza, when there were anglers every few yards on that famous stretch, a few miles upstream, on the middle Avon, coarse fishing was very restricted both in the numbers of anglers allowed on the water and the months when fishing was available. The middle Avon barbel had little or no experience of anglers' baits such as maggots or hemp, and consequently many regarded these barbel as very difficult to catch because they simply didn't recognize conventional baits as food. But by the 1980s, the middle Avon opened up to many more anglers and therefore more bait was introduced, especially maggots and casters in large quantities, and having weaned the barbel

on to their baits, these anglers caught the previously almost uncatchable barbel.

Even where barbel do have previous experience of a bait, it sometimes takes a while for them to switch on to taking it, especially where there is an abundance of natural food and they don't particularly need anything to supplement it. This is especially true of particle baits such as maggots and casters. Constant feeding for an hour or so may be needed before the barbel realize that this steady stream of particles is in fact a continuing food supply they can take advantage of. This is, of course, their natural, instinctive behaviour, because they attune to sudden explosions of food such as spawning minnows, caddis grubs on weed, migrating elvers and so on, so that once aware of these seasonal events they can take full advantage of them.

This focused feeding on many small items isn't the only way that barbel feed, and a single large food item trundling down the current can sometimes tempt them.

Baits for Barbel

The list of potential barbel baits is long, yet among these are a few consistent winners that keep on producing. The types of bait are best divided into several categories: naturals, particles, traditional, meat-based and modern, which will include pastes, pellets and boilies. There is

Despite the many alternatives, halibut pellets are currently the most popular barbel bait, both for feed and hookbait.

some cross-over here and there, but that shouldn't cause too many problems. Some baits are better suited to particular methods and conditions.

Natural Baits

Natural baits are those small creatures that barbel find naturally in the river; a variety of worms, caddis grubs, minnows and other small fish and brook lampreys are just a few examples. All of these baits will catch barbel, though it is arguable that many other baits will usually outfish them – except lobworms, which are an excellent bait when the water levels are up and

At the end of June each year it may be worth trying a minnow as bait when barbel take advantage of these small fish gathering on the shallows to spawn.

coloured, when barbel expect to find worms that have been washed from the banks by rising and then lowering levels. Barbel do succumb to those other natural baits, but their low rating in the barbel bait league table is more likely due to many anglers' reluctance to try them. None of them is selective; using minnows, for instance, will bring bites from chub, trout, perch and jack pike. To give yourself the best chance of success with them you need to use them at the right time of year (mid-June until the end of July) and in the right place – fast shallow water where you think or know barbel to be present. Search out the swim using a loafer float or rolling leger, lip-hooking the minnow on a size 6.

Alongside naturals, but obviously not found naturally in anywhere but the estuaries of rivers, we must place cockles, shrimps and prawns. You can purchase these fresh or frozen in fishmongers or supermarkets. It is vital to use them fresh, and they make an interesting change bait.

Although these natural baits are not always popular, don't dismiss them altogether: fishing is all about being prepared to experiment, and sometimes just succeeding with a different bait can be more satisfying than using the same old 'special'.

Particles

For many years particle baits have caught barbel, or at least persuaded barbel to feed, when introduced in sufficient quantities to trigger their basic instinct to capitalize on an abundance of one type of small food item. The disadvantages of particles can include high cost (at least in the case of maggot and caster), their non-selectiveness, and the difficulty of using hooks that are big and strong enough with some of the smallest particles such as hempseed.

Fortunately, we can overcome most of these disadvantages in various ways. Certainly modern hair-rigging methods coupled with superglue, used to glue the particles to the hair, can work miracles, although you should consider the sheer volume of work involved in doing this, and ask yourself if it's worth the time and the effort. Cost could be a more challenging problem, but mixing and matching cheaper particles with enough more expensive ones can allay this to a certain degree. The non-selectiveness of particles can often be mitigated through heavy and continuous feeding, to feed off most of the smaller species such as minnows, gudgeon and dace.

Maggots
There is no doubting the continuing attraction of maggots for barbel, though to make maggots work, particularly where large shoals of barbel are present, you will need plenty of them. In some prolific barbel swims that can mean a minimum of at least three or four pints, possibly more, even when combined with hemp, and a bait bill approaching £20 hardly makes for a cheap day's fishing. However, maggots remain a supreme barbel bait, especially if you are targeting a catch of barbel rather than one or two big fish. Maggots suit trotting, feeder tactics or simple legering with a bomb, although trotting a float through the swim and feeder fishing are the most likely methods to fully exploit fishing with particle baits. You can obtain maggots in all sorts of colours, but white maggots usually do as well as any for barbel.

Casters and Hemp
Although maggots are a good bait for barbel, casters can be even better, and in conjunction with hempseed as feed make for a deadly combination. Casters – the chrysalis stage of a fly's life cycle – are even more expensive than maggots, costing around 30 per cent more, but many anglers consider the cost is worth it as they have always been a very consistent barbel catcher. Two or three can be fished on a heavy gauge and therefore very strong size 14 hook. If a bigger hook is required to land bigger barbel, or any barbel that live close to snags, then you could always superglue casters to a hair rig on a bigger hook, although the time required to do that rather defeats the object of continually casting a feeder or sliding a float though a swim.

The combination of casters and hempseed is a very strong barbel feed trigger, and can keep barbel rooting in the swim for hours as the casters and tiny seeds wash into crevices in the gravel, the seed releasing the oil that barbel find almost irresistible. And as with maggots, you can use the hemp and caster combination for trotting, feeder fishing and legering.

The combination of hemp and caster remains a deadly mix for barbel.

Generally when fishing with casters it pays to have the freshest possible, and to look after them by keeping them refrigerated and in airtight bags to stop them developing further and becoming floaters. However, while you certainly don't want floaters, the need for ultra-fresh casters doesn't seem to apply to barbel. Many anglers over the years have found that old and stinking stale casters can be better than the freshest ones, which is the opposite case to, say, roach, when it's usual to use casters that are only a day or two changed from being a maggot. Whether it is the strong smell of old casters that makes the difference it's hard to say, and while sticking your nose into a bag of three-week-old casters isn't a pleasant experience, it certainly isn't a smell that deters barbel from feeding.

Hemp
Hemp fishing for barbel isn't popular because it is difficult to present hemp on a hook that is

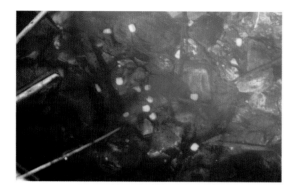

Seen here through a foot of water it's easy to spot the highly visible sweetcorn among the usual gravel and debris.

substantial enough to land a hard-fighting barbel. It can be done, but many anglers consider it is not worth the effort. One way is to superglue dried grains of cooked hemp to the hair, and perhaps one or two grains to the hook itself. When float fishing a size 14 or even a size 12 Drennan Super Specimen or Super Spade hook can be used, and a few grains superglued to it, with one grain of artificial hempseed threaded on to the hook. Anglers who have tried hemp fishing for barbel, including Graham, mainly through curiosity just to see if it would work, have come to the conclusion that, although it is an interesting exercise that does catch fish, there are far better methods that give a better return for much less effort.

Tares and Maple Peas

As many a roach angler has discovered when his next bite produced an unexpected and violent bend in the rod, often followed by the loud crack of a line breaking, barbel like tares just as much as big roach. The ideal conditions for hemp and tare fishing are in hot weather with high water temperatures, and the roach feeding activity attracts the barbel. Mark located some very big summer roach on the Dorset Stour at Longham some years ago in hot weather that had a liking for tares fished well over-depth on fine float tackle. Yet despite feeding very sparingly, just two or three tares every five minutes, the barbel inevitably muscled in after an hour or two. Maple peas are even larger than tares, and equally attractive.

Sweetcorn

Sweetcorn arrived on the angling scene in the early 1970s, and it wasn't long before many anglers found this sweet particle to be an excellent barbel bait. It has much going for it: a sweet flavour, cheap and easy to obtain, small enough to almost be classed as a particle, and barbel love it. Its drawback is that when barbel have been hammered on it a few times, its bright colour helps alert them to the fact that it spells danger; however, on waters where it hasn't been used much it still works. Occasionally on stretches where it has blown to such an extent that no one uses it any more, barbel have completely forgotten about its associated danger, and it can be used successfully again.

Traditional Baits

At one time both bread and cheese (or cheese paste) accounted for many barbel, partly through extensive use, and while there is always a chance of picking up a barbel using these baits, there are many better ones. However, don't ignore them completely, because bread-flake is an excellent barbel bait in winter on many rivers. Graham first discovered this on the Ribble when chub fishing with breadflake in winter. On the milder days there were times when he was catching more barbel than chub, and even when he changed to more traditional barbel baits, it was often still the case that the barbel preferred bread. Further trials on other rivers revealed that bread was a top winter barbel bait – not all the time, but enough to make it a 'must have' alternative bait when fishing certain rivers in winter.

Meat-Based Baits

Meaty baits have accounted for thousands of barbel in the last fifty years. The original meat-based baits were sausagemeat pastes and pieces of sausage. Many different meat paste recipes were also formulated, with their basis in cat and dog foods. Spices such as curry powder, turmeric and garlic were added, spices that remain firm favourites with barbel anglers to this day, although they are more likely to be added to boilie mixes. One of Graham's favourites was meatballs straight from the tin, and he even devised a method of hair-rigging them with a

A hair-rigged bait-banded meatball is an ideal bait for floodwater conditions.

Luncheon meat is a renowned barbel bait, and 'Bacon Grill' is a favourite brand as it stays on the hook well.

bait band. Meatballs are quite a soft bait and can easily be thrown off the hook when casting, but the bait-band method overcomes this problem.

However, the bait that had real potential was luncheon meat. Its texture is ideal in that it is soft enough to hook and hair-rig easily, yet tough enough to withstand casting – and at times retrieving, too. It can be used in many different sizes, from matchbox size on big hooks, to smaller cubes on smaller hooks, and you can use it straight from the tin without any preparation whatsoever other than cutting it into bait-sized pieces. Further variations on using meat include the similar Bacon Grill, which some anglers prefer as it stays on the hook better, and peperami or other spicy sausage variants. Meat baits can be hooked on as they are, or hair-rigged. Different brands of luncheon meat have different characteristics; some are softer and fattier, others are less fatty and firmer. It comes down to personal choice, though Plumrose chopped ham and pork, and Bacon Grill are two commonly used supermarket brands. There are also special flavoured luncheon meats available in tackle shops, and these are worth considering.

Although it is tempting and convenient to take tins of meat on to the river bank, you will find that many clubs ban anglers from taking

tins to the bank due to the risk to cattle cutting themselves on the discarded containers. It is better to remove the meat from the tin before fishing and to keep the meat in a bait box. In hot weather, meat can deteriorate quickly, so it is best to keep it cool in a coolbag out of the sun. In colder weather it is possible to freeze any remaining meat baits a couple of times.

The biggest problem with luncheon meat is that, like that other popular bait sweetcorn, it has been over-used to such an extent on many popular waters that it can actually spook the barbel on those days when they are not particularly hungry, especially a static piece of meat legered in clear water.

There are several ways to increase meat's effectiveness. First, use it in high water conditions when the barbel are more likely to be seeking food mainly by its smell. Second, in normal conditions use it as a rolling bait (this technique is covered in detail later in the book, *see* p. 115). Third, try pieces of meat torn from the block of meat instead of the usual neat cubes that you get from using a knife. And another way is to thread three or four smaller cubes of meat on the hair, rather than one big one. Also, consider giving the meat some special treatment to enhance its attractiveness, or just to change the usual flavour, texture and colour: frying cubes of meat is one option, as is dyeing it, or using

This barbel fell to a boilie.

other additives to change its flavour. Anything that changes the meat bait in appearance or flavour to allay at least some of the potential suspicion of wary barbel is worth a try.

Alternative Baits

Prawns, shrimps, cockles, mussels, crayfish, all have caught barbel at some time or other, as have more 'way out' offerings such as chips, small potatoes, various beans, peas: everything and anything edible could be worth a go – and who knows, you could just drop on something that is like the pot of gold at the end of the rainbow, that magic bait we're all looking for. Or there again, we can just realize that the best baits are usually the more tried, tested and proven ones, and the rest just small distractions to while away those hours when the tried and tested are not producing the goods. Never be

afraid to experiment, but also hope for – though never expect – the untried and untested to be the holy grail.

Modern Baits

It is hardly surprising that the wealth of knowledge built up in the last forty years in the carp world has had a knock-on effect on barbel fishing. The tremendous range of carp baits in modern tackle shops is hardly going to be missed by those seeking barbel. Furthermore, plenty of carp anglers enjoy trying for barbel, or have switched their allegiance from carp to barbel, and in doing so have brought their ideas and experience with carp baits to the barbel-fishing scene. The result has been a barbel fishing-bait revolution.

Pellets

Anglers have used trout pellets for coarse fishing for at least forty years, but it was in a five-year period from the mid-1990s onwards that their use for barbel fishing really took off. Initially, some anglers began using small trout pellets (3mm or 4mm) as a means of bulking out their feed when feeder fishing. These small pellets escape from swimfeeders just as well as maggots, casters and hempseed, yet are cheaper and easier to store than maggots and casters. It soon became clear that the barbel had grown accustomed to the pellets and that their use was improving anglers' results.

The big step was when much bigger pellets made of exactly the same mix became available. Manufactured for farm-bred halibut, these very rich and oily pellets are highly attractive to barbel, but instead of tiny pellets of just 3m or 4mm we had pellets of 15mm to 20 mm, and even larger – 'donkey chokers' in common parlance. By carefully drilling these bigger pellets it is possible to hair-rig them. As pellets began to be manufactured specifically for angling, the entire range of sizes became available, from micro pellets of just 1mm, up to 28mm. Furthermore different shapes, types, colours and flavours became available. Most pellets are hard, also 'expander' pellets that need preparation are available, but are difficult to keep on the hook or hair for long periods in flowing water. In later years a popular pellet has been one

This mix of dampened pellets is an ideal feeder filler for barbel.

Tying a bait band to the hair is one way of presenting a hard bait such as a halibut pellet.

made into an elliptical shape, though it is not radically different from any other pellet other than the shape.

Given the occasional difficulties that anglers have in drilling hard pellets (they split easily, especially if not very fresh), it's hardly surprising that there is a huge range of specialist pellet-type hookbaits available. Many of these are either ready drilled or of a tough, spongy consistency so they may be easily attached to a hair rig using a baiting needle. The alternative is to use a proprietary silicon bait band or two, or a bait band attached to a hair loop.

In addition there is a whole range of flavours, sizes and colours available.

Pastes

The idea of using pastes as bait is an old one; making bread paste from stale bread or flour dates back centuries, as does the idea of additives to make the paste more attractive. In more modern times cheese paste and sausage meat paste have both been popular barbel baits. The popularity of trout pellets gave rise to pastes made from ground-up pellets. Any boilie mix mixed up into a paste with eggs is a potential paste mix. This has been taken a step further, with specialist pastes designed to catch barbel. And whereas previously pastes were moulded on to the hook, many anglers now hair-rig a

pellet and mould the paste around that, or use the paste as a boilie wrap. These specialist pastes have been concocted for specific uses, such as cold weather winter fishing and floodwater as well as more normal conditions in summer and autumn.

Boilies

In pecking order, it is probably true to say that pellets are No. 1 on the list of modern barbel baits, with boilies coming a close second and pastes a poor third. Most of the time it won't make any difference at all to the barbel if you're using pellet or boilie, providing the bait is lying in the right spot on the riverbed at the right time. After all, the only real difference between a pellet and boilie is the shape and consistency, but where boilies are concerned, you can make these any shape and size and consistency you fancy.

As for boilie flavours, the usual savoury, meaty, fishy, spicy ones are usually best, but as always, never assume that is written in stone. Graham well remembers the time when small eels were a nightmare nuisance on the Ribble, when he fished fruity, sweet-flavoured boilies to avoid them and found that the barbel, at that time anyhow, actually preferred them to the standard savoury ones.

Boilies vary in size from 10mm to over 20mm, with 14mm or 15mm boilies being the

Because barbel mouth baits directly off the bottom, generally a much shorter hair is used than is usual for carp.

masala and tikka masala. Turmeric is a well proven barbel attractor especially luncheon meat lightly fried in it. Never be afraid to try any spicy flavour for barbel. Other known barbel flavours are garlic, any sea-food or fishy ones such as crab, and any meaty flavours such as liver. Then there is hemp oil, chilli oil and a whole lot more that are all worth a try.

Don't be Narrow-Minded

The smart angler will not rely totally on any one bait, but will be prepared to change from one to another according to the river he's fishing, the time of year, even the time of day, and the conditions at the time, whether clear or coloured water, high or low water, or sometimes just to see if the barbel will respond. The angler who declares he is either a pellet or a boilie man, or a sweetcorn or maggot man, will at times miss out, whereas the angler who is open-minded, carries a reasonable variety of baits, and is prepared to change according to prevailing conditions, will, most of the time, enjoy more consistent success.

standard size. But a good trick at times is to dispense with the large single boilie in favour of using two or more smaller ones, or even a single smaller one when the barbel are being especially cagey. Yet another little trick that can give you an edge is to trim the sides of a larger boilie with a knife, to give it four flat sides with rounded corners, so to speak. This makes it a different than the usual boilie and also releases more flavour into the current. It's also a good idea to carry a ball of the paste the boilies were made from to use as a wrap. You just mould a ball of the paste around the boilie; the paste will slowly dissolve and leak lots of little particles and flavour trails in the current, and hopefully lead the barbel straight to your bait.

Flavours for Barbel Baits

Savoury flavours are undoubtedly favourite for barbel and definitely for many barbel anglers, although barbel prefer a sweet or a fruit flavour more often than many barbel anglers realize. Most times, they have a pronounced preference for spicy flavours such as curry and garam

Feeding for Barbel

One of the challenges of fishing rivers is that, unlike stillwaters, feeding a swim is more difficult due to the river currents. Add the fact that many barbel waters have strong currents, and it is clear that we need to consider the problems of accurately feeding the swim. We need to:

- Understand the mechanics of delivering the feed to the bed of the river without scaring the fish.
- Know where to feed in the swim, taking into account the current.
- Know what to feed.
- Know how much to feed.
- Know how often to feed, or when to top up the feed.

Of these questions, the first one has the most straightforward answers.

The Mechanics of Feeding a Swim

At its simplest, we can introduce bait by hand or catapult. At short range and in moderately fast water, this may be completely satisfactory, and this method does form the mainstay of the trotting technique. So long as we are confident that the feed we are introducing is sinking reasonably quickly and hitting bottom at the spot that we want it to, then this method is ideal for trotting and some legering applications. Accuracy is important, and using a catapult increases the range at which you can feed. On some rivers, the barbel are immediately below the tail of large weedbeds. In this instance, it is sometimes possible to feed on top of the weedbed so that the feed filters down through the weedbed itself. If you are feeding different types of bait together such as maggots and hemp, or casters and hemp, or hemp and tares, you need to make allowance for the different sink rates of the two baits. Of maggots, casters, tares and hemp, maggots sink the slowest, followed by casters, then hemp, and then tares as the fastest sinker. Pellets are more variable; larger pellets tend to sink the fastest. Throwing in a handful or two of bait in the margins before feeding the swim will give you an idea of sink rates when trying baits you haven't used before.

Feeding by Hand

Hand feeding does tend to spread the feed over a large area and relies on being able to get the feed to sink quickly without it washing out of the swim before it has hit bottom. It is clear that although it has its uses, there are some drawbacks as well.

Feeding by Catapult

A catapult can also tend to spread the feed more than we would wish, but is usually a tighter feed than by hand. Make sure you use the right catapult pouch and elastic to suit the bait you're feeding.

Bait Droppers

Using a bait dropper overcomes many of the problems with hand feeding, and enables you to deposit lots of bait with great accuracy on the bottom. It is ideal for laying a bed of hemp in a swim. Bait droppers come in several sizes, and it

A large bait dropper like this one is ideal for getting a bed of bait down at close range; this one has been painted a drab green to camouflage it.

is the larger ones that barbel anglers find most useful. It can be useful to set up a spare rod just for using a bait dropper. It is best to use bait droppers at close range, say, up to about fifteen yards out; obtaining accurate positioning of your bait beyond this range is difficult, to say the least.

Swimfeeders

Swimfeeders overcome some of the problems with loose feeding and bait droppers. Provided your casting is accurate and the chosen feeder is able to hold position as it deposits its load, a swimfeeder is an excellent means of accurate and regular feeding. On waters where a constant

A big purpose-made, open-end swimfeeder that's ideal for getting plenty of bait down on the riverbed.

These pre-tied PVA mesh bags are full of dry pellet mix.

stream of bait is required, usually where the barbel are found in substantial shoals, this is the key to success. It is vital to use a swim-feeder that will hold bottom throughout the emptying period and remain in place when it is fully empty. There is no point in laying that trail of feed only for the bait to roll out of the swim when the feeder is empty and there-fore lighter. It is better to fish a heavier than necessary feeder rather than one that moves when empty.

Adapted Carp Methods

Barbel anglers have borrowed several feeding methods from their carp fishing colleagues. The first one is an adaptation of feeder fishing but using a Method feeder with a groundbait and particle mix. The second one, a very popular tactic, is to attach small PVA bags to the hook or leger weight to deposit pellets and boilies around the hookbait. And finally, you can use PVA string to attach stringers of pellets or boilies to your weight.

What to Feed

The idea of any angler feeding the swim is to attract and hold fish in that swim, and ideally to get them to feed with such confidence that you allay any wariness they may have and give you a good chance of catching them. Barbel fishing is no different, and given the fast-flowing nature of many barbel swims, special consideration is needed to determine what to feed. In general terms we are looking for bait samples similar to what will be used on the hook. There are exceptions such as hempseed, a very good holding bait that will often keep barbel active in an area for hours while we try to tempt them with larger fare. Casters are also a good holding bait.

With some baits, especially boilies, it can pay to crumble up the bait samples so that when the barbel finds the hook offering it finds the larger morsel more attractive.

Prebaiting

The concept of prebaiting exists to achieve several things: to get the fish used to finding bait in a particular swim, to wean them away from natural food and on to a bait that otherwise they may fail to recognize as food, and to increase their confidence in a food supply that (at least during the prebaiting period) offers no danger and appears to be constantly present in abundance. Barbel are notoriously slow on the uptake in recognizing new baits, and prebaiting offers a way to speed this up. It is

usually unnecessary to use vast quantities of bait to do this, unless the target is a huge shoal of barbel, but instead concentrate on the regular introduction of a few samples of bait. Clearly such an approach is likely to work best on relatively small, lightly fished waters. On very heavily fished waters such as the Royalty Fishery on the Hampshire Avon there is so much bait going in on a daily basis that the barbel are weaned on to whatever the majority of anglers are using. It is only when an angler or group of anglers has persevered with a new bait that eventually the new bait replaces the previous bait fad.

Looking After Your Bait

The quantities of bait required for barbel fishing are significant; however, careful storage of bait bought in bulk can cut the cost of barbel fishing. A freezer is useful for fresh frozen boilies, pastes, unused meat baits and particles such as hemp, sweetcorn and tares, which can be prepared in bulk and split into bags. Pellets and boilies with a certain shelf-life are best kept in a sealed container with a close-fitting lid to keep out sunlight and vermin such as mice and rats. Most of these baits are all right for up to twelve months, but beyond this, the quality of the flavour may deteriorate. It may be worth writing the purchase date on bags so that you know how long you've had them.

RIGHT: *Barbel caught on halibut pellet.*

BELOW: *These green and betaine-flavoured micro pellets are a popular feedbait for barbel.*

5 TACKLE: RODS, REELS AND LINES

Rods

The modern barbel angler is spoilt for choice when it comes to tackle; there is a great variety of rods from many of our major manufacturers, and not a few from cottage industries who make their own custom-built versions to the individual angler's specifications. Although quite a number of barbel anglers prefer the traditional route and use built cane rods coupled with centrepin reels, there is no doubt that a top quality, modern carbon-fibre rod is the personal choice for the majority. However, most of the traditionalists will be the first to admit that the antiquated tackle they use is not because they consider it to be the most efficient, but because they get the most fun from it. The tackle and methods you enjoy using most should always be your first consideration, as fishing is not all about what catches the most and the biggest.

However, the tackle recommended in this book will be the most up to date – though by all means go down the traditionalist route at a later date if that is what you prefer.

Where rods are concerned, it is very much a case of matching the tool to the job, in that different venues and different conditions have different demands. Dropping a light rig under your feet into a small stream for average-sized barbel needs a very different rod to one capable of casting a huge feeder loaded with up to 8oz of lead into the middle of the tidal Trent with three feet of floodwater raging through. Pulling a big barbel away from the sanctuary of a sunken tree again needs sufficient power to match a heavy line. Yet that same rod might be totally unsuited to a lightweight roving approach. And so far that only covers legering techniques, because when it comes to float fishing for barbel, yet another type of rod has to be considered – although it

Legering for barbel on the Wye.

must be said that the majority of your barbel fishing will be legering because most barbel swims lend themselves better to a legered bait, and most often you will be playing a waiting game.

Regardless of any other consideration though, the first choice you make is the strength of the line you need for a particular situation. Then, and only then, do you select a rod that will match correctly with that line to land the fish. For instance, if you decide that you need a 12lb line to bully a big barbel away from snags, then this considerably narrows down your choice of rod. So, line choice first, rod choice second.

A barbel rod needs four main features:

- The power to handle whatever line you consider necessary to land the biggest fish you are likely to encounter in a particular river or swim.
- The strength to cast the terminal tackle, along with whatever that terminal tackle is loaded with to feed the fish – say, a heavy feeder or a large leger weight and possibly a PVA bag of feed.
- An action that includes a not-too-heavy tip section to indicate the less-than-savage bites that occasionally occur.
- And as important as any other factor, it must feel right to you. If a rod ticks all the other three boxes but feels in any way awkward or clumsy, then pick up another one until you find one you're happy with.

One characteristic that a good barbel rod should possess is the ability to absorb those terrific lunges that barbel are capable of when they pick up the bait and take off downstream, and those times during the fight when they decide to turn round and head for the sea or the nearest snag. Those explosive surges can easily result in your tackle getting smashed – yet a rod with the right action, powerful but flexible, combined with a correctly set drag on a fixed spool reel, or a well controlled centrepin reel, should mitigate this.

Test Curves
One of the ways by which rods are categorized is by test curve. The test curve of a rod is a means

This is the moment when a top class barbel rod has enough reserve to counter a final lunge.

of giving a rough guide to its power. It never has been an exact science, and is less so with modern high modulus carbon blanks, and despite two different rods having exactly the same test curve their action might be very different. How a rod bends is important; a rod that bends mainly in the tip section is said to be 'fast tapered', whereas one that bends throughout its length is said to be 'through action'.

In the early days of barbel fishing anglers used 'Avon'-type rods, which had a through action and a test curve of about a pound. If they were targeting big barbel in especially snaggy territory they'd step up to a carp rod with a test curve of 1.5lb. Since those far-off days several decades ago, the average barbel is considerably bigger and we fish for them using much stronger

The fighting curve of this standard barbel rod is well illustrated.

tackle. The ones we are mostly interested in have test curves between 1.5lb and 2lb. This range covers most situations between 'standard' barbel fishing for fish up to 7lb or so in open water, to hauling the big boys away from snags. If you need anything heavier than this, for use in large, fast and possibly flood-swollen rivers where the extra strength is needed to cast the huge weights required to hold bottom, the choice falls in the carp rod range.

As a very rough but still somewhat useful guide, the ideal line for a rod usually has a breaking strain of about five times the test curve. There is plenty of room for leeway on this, especially at the upper end, so that a rod with a test curve of 1.75lb (the modern standard for barbel rods) would be ideally matched to 9lb line, would cope with 6lb line, yet be easily capable of contending with 12lb line, such is the tolerance factor of a modern carbon-fibre rod. Dr Stephen Harrison of Harrison Advanced Rods, like Daiwa, one of the few rod blank designers and manufacturers in the UK, is also of the opinion that the test curve system is flawed. He says:

> In practice the problem of pulling tips to 90 degrees with a 90-degree pull probably seemed academic with a cane Avon or Mk IV carp rod. The test curve method worked in a practical sense for flexible and forgiving cane rods. But as rods have become more powerful and materials have changed from cane through glass to carbon, the problems of measurement have increased dramatically. The high modulus tip of the modern rod is more reluctant to follow the line to 90 degrees.

One does wonder if there is some other guide we can use that will give us a more accurate idea of the playing *and* casting power of a rod, and also a good idea of its action. Dr Harrison wonders the same thing, and says:

> In the past I have discussed this problem with many people, but so far none has come up with a solution. What we need is a measure of how much line a rod gives during flexing as a result of a pull by a fish. Imagine a rod clamped in a fixed position so that we could measure

Measuring Test Curve

To measure the test curve (TC) of a rod, the butt, with reel fitted, is fixed horizontally. The line is threaded through the rings, and sufficient weight added to the line to load up the rod until the tip is at an angle of 90 degrees to the butt. The weight required to do that – the loading, usually in pounds (lb) and ounces (oz) – is the test curve, and multiplying the test curve of the rod by a factor of five gives you the nominal figure for the casting weight in ounces and the line strength in pounds. For instance, a rod with a 2lb TC will cast a weight up to 2oz and handle a line up to 10lb, although modern carbon-fibre rods will cast weights and bend well beyond the nominal test curve factor, making them immensely versatile. Nevertheless, the test curve is still a useful unit for giving us a rough guide to the power of a rod.

This powerful purpose-built barbel rod is capable of the most demanding barbel fishing situations.

deflection against force of pull. If we were to plot on a graph the amount of line given, or deflection of a rod, against pull or load, we would get a curve. This curve would vary from rod to rod according to the action. If we can find a simple way to describe this curve, then we would have a measure that indicated both power and action. The curve of deflection against load would have a faster rate of change, a steeper ramping up, than a through-action rod which would be closer to a straight line.

Different manufacturers try to get round the problem in different ways. Some stick to the old test curve, others describe their rods as being 'suitable for lines of xlb bs', while yet others say a rod will cast a weight up to xlb. None of them tells us exactly what we want to know – that is, casting and pulling power and action. For now, therefore, the test curve rating is still the best, although rough, guide. Experienced anglers will, as always, visit a large tackle shop and have a feel of a range of rods in the class they are looking for, and choose one that feels right to them. This is a non-scientific way of choosing a rod, but is still the one that will most

probably result in the angler selecting a rod that is fit for purpose.

Why the Difference in Cost?

A quick glance through the tackle adverts in the press or on the Internet will reveal that barbel rods can be obtained for as little as £30, though the cheap ones are usually around £50, and from there through all the price ranges up to in excess of £200. They can't all be the same quality, so what is the essential difference?

The blank is the principal component of a rod, which is usually made from a carbon-fibre composite. The carbon-fibre quality varies enormously: in simple terms the finer the carbon cloth, the more expensive it is. The better rods are made from cloth that is more expensive. The very cheapest rods are made from a cloth that is a mixture of carbon fibre and glass fibre, and the very cheapest might best be described as glass-fibre rods as they contain only enough carbon for it to be legal for them to say they are a carbon composite. Even some mid-range rods that cost between £50 and £100 have significant glass-fibre content. The giveaway on this is the weight of the rod: a rod made from a

This standard barbel rod will pack down into two pieces that are slightly more than 6ft long (approximately 2m), and therefore may not fit easily into a small car.

high grade of carbon fibre is very light, and this applies to all rods – match rods, carp rods, fly rods, barbel rods; as the proportion of glass fibre increases, so does the wall thickness of the tube, and so therefore does the weight.

In addition to the quality of carbon fibre used, the taper of the rod and how well that taper has been designed also changes the quality of the rod. The compromise between casting (fast taper) and playing (slow taper) must be reached. Here the better quality of the carbon fibre plays another part. When you cast you impart a lot of energy into the rod, which is released during the cast. Top class carbon does this very efficiently, and the poorer quality ones much less so. This means that a better rod can help you cast more accurately and with less effort. Another significant factor that makes the difference between a top class rod and a cheaper one is that the power tolerance becomes greater, in that the best quality rods will handle a wider range of lines for a given breaking strain.

Length and Configuration

The vast majority of barbel rods are 12ft long and made in two pieces; a few are 11ft long.

For most barbel fishing, 12ft long rods are ideal; their only significant disadvantage is that because they are made in two pieces that are slightly longer than 6ft in length, it may be difficult to get them into a small car.

A common configuration for Avon and barbel rods is to have two tops, one a standard, and the other either a built-in quivertip or a quivertip carrier with a selection of quivertips to slot in. For true barbel rods with a test curve of 1.5lb or 1.75lb it is arguable whether the quivertip top is really necessary, and whether you'd be better off having a better quality rod with just the plain top. To explain this, consider two rods both costing £100: if one has an extra top with quivertips and the other doesn't, it is likely that the one with the extra top and quivertips is built from a lower quality carbon fibre to compensate for the build cost of the extra top and quivertips.

Avon rods with a typical test curve of 1.25lb will also have these extra quivertip tops. In this instance it's worth considering, because you may well use such a rod for other types of fishing such as chub fishing where a quivertip may well offer a substantial advantage.

A further combination is to have two plain tops but with different test curve ratings, such as 1.75lb and 2lb. The big question mark over such rods is whether the rod is truly 'right' in one of its configurations. Because of the through-actioned nature of barbel rods the action of the butt section needs to match the top section, but if the rating is altering so much that may not be true, so you'd be better off buying two separate rods if you feel that you really need a heavier or lighter-actioned rod.

For feeder fishing and lightweight work there are also many feeder rods on the market. These are usually 11–13ft long, and classified as light, medium, heavy and extra heavy. The ones most likely to be usable for barbel fishing are medium and heavy ratings. A medium feeder rod usually translates into a test curve of about 1–1.25lb, and a heavy feeder as 1.25–1.5lb. Given that there is a quivertip in the end, attempting to measure the test curve of a feeder rod accurately is tricky. Feeder rods are designed to be much more casting tools than playing tools, but the better ones – often costing more than £100 – will not only cast well, but will also go some way towards having the prerequisite playing action due to the quality of the blank.

So bear in mind that feeder rods usually have a fast taper action to make it easier to cast a feeder to long range and pick up line on the strike, but that both of those design factors are somewhat redundant on a barbel rod, since most rivers are not that wide, and most barbel bites don't need to be struck at. However, the consequence of this particular fast taper design factor is that the rod as a fish-playing tool is considerably compromised, being prone to 'bottoming out' – reaching the full extent of its 'bendability' and therefore losing its shock absorber facet. So it pays to beware of this, and to take a good look at barbel rods with quiver-tips rather than a dedicated feeder rod if you decide that you do indeed want a barbel rod with a quivertip.

Matching the Rod to the Job

There are number of approaches to barbel fishing, and there is no perfect rod that suits them all, but below are a few pointers on the best choice for each:

General feeder fishing for shoal barbel (fish from 3–5lb): A good quality medium feeder rod or Avon-type rod with the quivertip option that should handle 6–8lb line and barbel up to 8lb. In choosing a rod for this type of fishing, consider whether you could be under-gunned due to other possibilities. Are you likely to encounter the occasional barbel that is much bigger than the average size of barbel you're tackled up for? Are you fishing close to snags, or bolt holes that the barbel will try to reach and

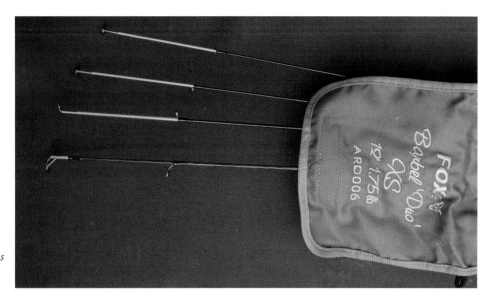

This versatile barbel rod has a standard top plus a carrier section for quivertips.

This purpose-built float rod has tamed plenty of barbel.

where a more powerful rod will serve you better?

Small river big barbel: A minimum specification for this type of fishing is a 1.75lb test curve rod, possibly a 2lb test curve, and capable of pulling a big barbel away from snags with 12lb line. Most modern barbel rods in this power range are designed for this sort of fishing.

Big river heavy feeder fishing: Either a 2lb test curve barbel rod or a light carp rod with a 2.25 or 2.5lb test curve should be man enough for this tough work. No need for quivertips! Such a rod is also ideal for floodwater fishing on big rivers such as the Severn where you may need as much as 8oz of lead to hold bottom.

Roving: A lightweight rod with no quivertip is ideal; as you'll be holding it most of the time, weight is more of a consideration than when the rod spends most of its time in rod rests.

The Harrison Interceptor, designed by Graham for long-range tench and bream fishing, is a versatile tool that is ideal for roving. It is 12 feet long with a test curve of 1lb 10oz, extremely light, and rolling meat expert Ray Wilton used this rod at one time for this style of fishing.

Rod Rings, Handles and Other Fittings
Most barbel rods have excellent ringing arrangements using top quality rings. The inserts for the rings may be silicon carbide (SiC), aluminium oxide or titanium oxide. While the SiC inserts are the most expensive, they are the most prone to developing line-shredding hairline cracks.

As for the reel fittings, perhaps the best advice is that it is worth checking that the reels you intend to use fit the rod snugly and securely, but up- or down-locking, screwed reel fittings are now pretty much standard. Daiwa use an unusual configuration on their rods with a flattened section on the handle that fits under your forearm and is very comfortable.

The high gloss finish on many barbel rods will reflect the sun, and on a clear river the reflections could be enough to scare the barbel. A coat of durable matt varnish will fix the problem, as will a gentle rub with wirewool, being careful only to reduce the gloss and not rub through the varnish to the bare blank.

Most anglers attach little importance to the handle length of a rod, yet it can make a tremendous difference to how the rod performs and to how it feels. Longer handles are necessary for long casting, to give you the extra leverage required to accelerate the rod tip through the casting arc and therefore throw the terminal tackle to greater distance. Yet a long handle is rarely, if ever, necessary for a river rod, unless of course you're fishing an extremely wide river and need to cast to the far bank. In reality that is highly unlikely. A handle of around 24–26in (60–65cm) is about right for a barbel rod, which will be short enough for you to be able to easily pass the rod in front of you when playing a fish, and a shorter handle for those shorter casts will go some way towards maintaining accuracy. Also, a small but nevertheless worthy little point is that a short handle will allow you to hold the rod more comfortably under your forearm and along your thigh when you're sat holding the rod and waiting for a bite.

ABOVE: *This Shimano Stradic 4000 is a perfect all-round reel.*

RIGHT: *The left hand eases the strain on the rod arm when barbel are charging off.*

Reels

There are three options when it comes to reels for barbel fishing; standard fixed spool reels, fixed spool reels with a free-spool facility, and centrepin reels. Most barbel fishing is carried out at comparatively short range – less than twenty yards – so that generally reels designed for long casting aren't required. This partly explains the enthusiasm for centrepin reels. The only possible exception to this is for long-range feeder fishing on big rivers where a cast of fifty yards or more could be required.

Whatever reel you choose, it pays to go for top quality. Barbel fishing can be tough on tackle, especially reels, when you could be constantly retrieving heavy feeders through equally heavy currents. Although you should make the rod do the work by pumping the feeder back and then winding the slack, there is still a certain amount of strain taken by the reel. A well built, robust reel should never let you down despite the hammering it will get, so that when you hook that barbel of a lifetime you can be sure it won't jam.

Standard Fixed Spool Reels

There are four sizes of reel that interest the barbel angler; in Daiwa and Shimano (two of the major brands) terms, these are designated 2500, 3500, 4000 and 5000. The smaller size can be used for lines to 8lb, though it is better for finer lines such as 4lb and 6lb which, it must be said, won't be used very often for barbel fishing unless you find a shoal of smaller fish in snag-free water. The advantage of the smaller size of reel is for trotting, being too small for most barbel legering situations. Standard barbel gear is better matched with the 4000 or 5000 size of reel. Such a reel is too large for comfortable trotting because your forefinger controlling the line as it peels off may struggle to reach the lip of the spool; a well designed 2500 size is better for this.

Whichever reel you use, buy the best you can afford. Barbel fishing is punishing for any reel, especially feeder fishing, and although plenty of cheap reels have lots of flash and even several ball bearings, the inferior material they are often made from usually means they have a very limited lifespan.

One consideration when buying modern fixed spool reels is whether to have one with a front or rear drag. It is claimed that the front drags are more sensitive, but given that you will have the drag fairly well screwed down anyway, then a good rear drag should do the job just as well. One advantage with one range of Shimano rear drag reels is that they have a 'Fightin' Drag', which enables you to reduce or increase the drag setting with a lever by plus or minus 30 per cent while playing a fish, and without changing the original drag setting. As this is at the rear of the reel, you don't get your fingers near the line while playing the fish, which is a further advantage of rear drag reels. Rear drag reels weigh slightly more than similar model front drag reels, but with most types of barbel fishing this isn't a significant factor.

Free-Spool Fixed Spool Reels

Free-spool reels, known colloquially as Baitrunners – which is actually a Shimano trademark – are excellent for barbel fishing, for the extremely sudden and violent bite a barbel most often gives can easily catch you unawares, especially when you fish some way through the dark hours and a long spell without any activity leads to you dozing off. The safety margin of the free-spool is a godsend in such a situation, and many barbel anglers use the free-spool facility as a matter of course, because they know that just a moment's distraction can lead to a rod taking a nosedive into the river.

Free-spool reels in the smaller carp-fishing sizes, 4000–5000, are the usual choice: these are plenty big enough, and the best quality ones are robust enough to take all the strain demanded by big feeder fishing on big rivers, as well as meeting all the requirements of most other types of barbel fishing on most rivers.

One type of reel that is certainly too big for barbel fishing is the 'big pit' type of free-spool reel; however, a recent development by Shimano has given us 'mini' big pit reels, which combine the power and line capacity of big pit reels with much smaller dimensions and less weight. One of these reels could well be suitable for this heavyweight fishing due to their sheer robustness and exceptional cranking power. Big rivers with several feet of floodwater powering through, when feeders weighing up to 8oz or so are demanded, are ideal situations for the 'mini' big pit-type reel.

Centrepin Reels

Many barbel anglers consider centrepin reels to be ideal for their style of fishing, and this has long been the case. A good proportion of barbel fishing is done at close range, and so the main disadvantage of centrepin reels – restricted casting range – is largely mitigated. For close-in legering and trotting a centrepin reel has its advantages: the direct contact with the fish when playing, and even the use of the ratchet as a bite alarm when legering. Trotting for barbel is different to other forms of trotting, where in many cases a small, well designed fixed spool reel is often superior. Barbel trotting tends to be at close range and more a form of slowly trundling the float through the swim, and a centrepin reel is ideal for this style. For waggler fishing it has serious drawbacks, and the same also applies to long-range feeder tactics.

The bottom line is that centrepin fishing puts the control of your tackle and the playing of the fish back into your own hands: no drags except the pressure that can be applied with your thumb or fingers, and no gears to multiply the

A free spool reel like this Shimano Baitrunner is a versatile reel for legering on big rivers.

turns of the spool. This ultimate control may not suit everyone, but for those who want it, there is no other reel that can offer it in quite the same way.

Most important is that using a centrepin for barbel fishing can be good fun, and there is no better reason for using one.

However, it's important to understand the different types of centrepin that are around. First of all it's worth pointing out that many modern 'pins are not true centrepins, because instead of a pin they have a ball bearing. These are noisier than a true pin but do the job well enough if lubricated correctly. The next thing is that there are several types of centrepin reel, each being especially suited to certain styles of fishing. The first type is the traditional caged 'pin such as the Rapidex or Trudex. These reels can be purchased for about £50 upwards, and are robust, dependable workhorses. They are nothing special for trotting although usable, but are best for close-in legering where their check is perfect for bite detection. These reels are compact with a small spool and lightweight design, but are very practical for close-in fishing.

The next type is the uncaged trotting reel. There are many versions, but among the best are Adcock Stanton reels. These do not generally have a check but are first class for trotting. In recent years, Okuma have produced some fine trotting reels in this style, and of course there are a number of very fine reels that J. W. Young have produced, including developments from the original Aerial and Match Aerial reels – excellent but pricey. One reasonable option is to get an old Speedia. These old reels are a bit of a workhorse, and are sought after for practical purposes rather than collectability; they remain reasonably priced in the second-hand market.

A more recent development has been of solidly built reels specifically for barbel fishing. These reels are not designed for fine lines in the way of the original pattern centrepins, but are much more robust, and ideal for 10lb line; however they are not the best for trotting. They do have an excellent check. A good example is the Kingpin.

The final type of 'pin is totally different in that it is the type of reel that is a centrepin when you wind in, and a fixed spool when you cast –

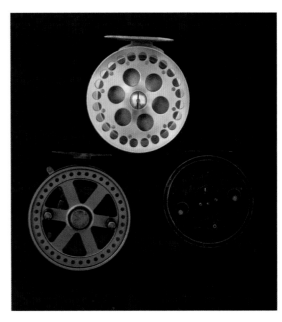

This small selection of centrepin reels includes a specialized trotting reel: Adcock Stanton (top), a robust reel; Kingpin (bottom left); and a traditional reel, Rapidex (bottom right).

in other words a side caster, where the spool is turned through 90 degrees. Very few have ever been made that are really up to the job, although the Ray Walton one is something special – but then it ought to be at over £300.

Whichever centrepin you choose, it is worth checking that it fits the reel seat on your rods. The latest centrepin reels are generally all right in this respect, but some older reels were designed in the days of sliding reel fittings and their over-large feet don't fit the modern screw-down fittings. Centrepins are less robust in some respects than fixed spool reels; they certainly get damaged if dropped on a hard surface, and it is best to keep grit and bait particles out of the works.

Lines

There are mixed views when it comes to reel lines for barbel fishing. The choice comes down to braid or monofilament, and there are strong advocates for both. Just to complicate matters,

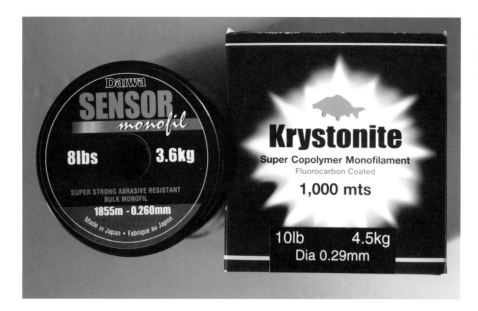

These two main lines in various breaking strains will cope with most barbel fishing situations.

the term 'monofilament' covers several types of line, each with its own characteristics. The biggest differences between braid and mono are as follows:

- Braid has very little stretch, perhaps 1 per cent, whereas mono has much more – from 10 to 20 per cent.
- Braid is very 'direct'; every tremble and pull is transmitted. Mono absorbs some of these more subtle indications.
- The lack of stretch with braid can lead to hook pulls and needs to be compensated for by flexibility in the rod.
- Braid can abrade easily.
- Braid has a tendency to float.
- Most practitioners of braid use it in 30lb test; if you get snagged it can be difficult to pull for a break.
- Braid is much more expensive than mono.

For the vast majority of barbel fishing a good, reliable, standard monofilament line is ideal as a main line. It is tough enough, cheap enough and sinks well enough to do all we ask. Its extra quality is that its stretch will play a part in providing extra shock absorption when playing barbel.

We need to be aware of two other types of monofilament line. The first type is the modern *copolymer* line, which has a low diameter compared to its breaking strength. However, copolymer lines are not as tough as regular nylon monos. While copolymer lines are useful for many coarse fishing applications, barbel fishing is not one of them. There are better ways to achieve the same advantages without sacrificing toughness.

The second type is *fluorocarbon*. This is made of a very different material to conventional nylon lines, so it has some fundamental differences. The first one is that its refractive index (ability to bend light) is much closer to that of water than conventional nylon, which, in theory at least, makes it much harder for fish to spot in water. Second, it is much stiffer than nylon and therefore more difficult to knot, though with care and the use of the correct knots that difficulty can be overcome. Finally, it is denser than nylon and will lie on the bottom better than nylon. It is rarely used as a reel line.

Hook links

Hook-length material takes four forms: mono, braid, coated or skinned braid, and fluorocarbon:

- Mono is tough, smooth, reliable, has a little stretch, and is quite good for lying straight on the bottom.

- Braid has a low diameter for its strength, is soft and supple, and reliable where there are no sharp objects likely to be encountered.
- Skinned or coated braid, with the skin stripped back from the hook for a few inches to expose the soft and supple braid beneath, has all the advantages of regular braid, but added stiffness and some protection from sharp objects.
- Fluorocarbon is less visible to the fish, is stiffer than regular mono, is very smooth, and lies flat to the bottom much better than any of the latter. There is a debate as to its toughness, however, the authors are from the pro-fluoro school, which believes that a top quality fluoro such as Kryston's Incognito is as reliable as any mono.

A selection of hook link materials.

The choice of hook length from the above is very much down to personal choice, and each exponent of a particular type will have very good reasons for his choice. If in any doubt go for regular mono and then put the rest through a trial period until you can judge for yourself. There is an argument that says it doesn't make a lot of difference what you use, if you use it correctly, to present a bait in the right place at the right time!

This is the moment when being able to hold the landing net steady in the current is vital.

6 TACKLE: OTHER GEAR

As with most aspects of modern angling, there is a vast array of accessories available for barbel fishing; some are essential, others less so, and how important they are depends on the type of fishing. Float-fishing tackle is covered in Chapter 10.

Landing Gear

Landing Net Head

Barbel are sizeable fish. Unlike carp, they are relatively slim but long, so although a carp can weigh four times as much as a barbel, it is quite acceptable to use a standard carp landing net of 42in (106cm). Big barbel are in the region of 30–32in (75–80cm) in length, although they may vary considerably in weight according to individual depth. Beware though, for many standard carp landing nets have a bowstring front cord and a micro-mesh or carp sack material bottom to the mesh, which is fine in a lake but will cause problems on a powerful river. Such a net is certainly big enough, but on many barbel waters it will create more problems than it solves.

The big difference between barbel fishing and carp fishing is that there is every chance we will be attempting to land the barbel in fast-flowing water. Add in the problem that it may be weedy as well, and it is clear that in many circumstances a carp net is likely to be too unwieldy to use, especially if you are trying to manage it single-handed. In a strong current, the flow pushing against the micromesh will make it impossible to hold the net steady with one hand, let alone manoeuvre it if needs be. We may also need to be able to push weed out of the way, which is another drawback of the bowstring net.

Fortunately the perfect nets for barbel fishing do exist. A deep spoon-type net with a frame of at least 27in (68cm) and a deep large mesh is easy to handle in fast water, even single-handed. Although it doesn't seem possible, provided the net is deep it doesn't matter if the net frame is not as long as a big barbel: it will slide into it with no real problem. Spoon landing nets of 30in (75cm) are also available for those anglers targeting outsize fish. The depth of the mesh is important for two reasons: initially to safely cradle the fish when it is lifted from the water, and secondly to offer it the relative comfort of a sling where it can recover from an energy-sapping fight. Barbel fight so hard they may not have enough energy to swim off when they are returned to the water, and most barbel anglers will hold the fish either in the water at the river's edge, or if the banks are not safe enough to do that, in the landing net in the margins while it recovers.

Landing Net Handle

As well as a good net you need a strong, and often long, landing net handle. Consider the type of waters you fish. On some rivers the banks are low and make it easy to get to a fish for netting, but on others they are steep and difficult. Bear in mind that there will be times when you have to move away from your fishing position to land a fish some way up or downstream due to the current, weed and other snags immediately in front of your swim. In particular when you fish rivers with steep banks down to the water – especially on those days following floods when the water has receded, leaving muddy and dangerously slippery banks – you will need a strong and long landing net handle. A standard carp-fishing landing net handle is 6ft (2m) in length, which is too short for most river banks. Look for the telescopic ones that extend to around 10ft (3m), yet still have the necessary stiffness. Avoid the put-over type extending landing net handles as these are not safe to use on a sloping river bank, the risk being that the sections can pull apart and the hapless fish will slide back into the river, still enclosed in the net. You may still be able to play it, but how will you land it?

As an aside, never take chances on those steep and slippery river banks. If your own safety and the safety of the fish is in any doubt whatsoever, find a safer swim.

Unhooking Mat

Having successfully landed your barbel, it is good practice to use a wet unhooking mat. As it is likely on some days that you will be walking a fair distance, you need one that packs away compactly yet does the job adequately. Such a mat will protect the barbel against any sharp or rough objects on the riverbank while you unhook it. Furthermore, a number of roving barbel anglers use their unhooking mat as a cushion to sit on while fishing, so they don't need to carry a fold-up chair.

Scales

A reliable set of scales is a 'must' for any angler who wants to record accurately the weight of the fish he catches. Most of us have targets, and for many barbel anglers it is the capture of a double-figure (10lb-plus) fish. Any fish that looks to be around or over that weight can be weighed and recorded. Despite the electronic and digital revolution, there is still something to be said for a reliable set of dial scales that are tough and never need batteries – although a quality set of digital scales will give superior accuracy and a readout that can be illuminated in darkness.

ABOVE: *A spoon-type net is ideal for most barbel fishing.*

BELOW: *Sometimes it is advantageous to unhook a barbel in the water.*

These digital scales are Graham's choice of scales for fishing.

ABOVE: *This weigh sling is ideal for big barbel.*

BELOW: *Having everything to hand when unhooking a barbel makes the process much quicker; here we have unhooking mat, forceps, weigh sling and scales all ready.*

Unhooking Gear

Besides the unhooking mat you will need a set of forceps and a large barrel-type disgorger. If you float fish for smaller barbel with hooks less than a 14, then a standard barrel-type disgorger will also be needed.

Terminal Tackle

Hooks

The modern barbel angler is spoilt for choice when it comes to suitable hooks, no matter what style of fishing is involved, as there are strong, sharp hooks in many patterns. Generally, forged short-shanked hooks with in-turned points find favour for most barbel fishing. For float fishing the normal practice is to use spade-end hooks, but given that the knot will be extremely tested, it is probably safest to use similar eyed hooks to avoid the sharp spade cutting through the line. Fortunately, the popularity of match fishing for single-figure carp on commercial fisheries has created a strong market for small, strong, eyed hooks, so there is plenty of choice.

One thing to watch out for when barbel fishing is that it is easy to blunt a hook, as it is constantly dragged across gravelly bottoms. Check the hook whenever you re-cast, and sharpen or replace it if it is blunt.

Leads

There is a tackle-grabbing swim on the River Dane in Cheshire where one angler uses car wheel nuts, given to him by a car mechanic friend, instead of proprietary lead weights. The swim isn't hard to land barbel from, but is very hard on the pocket as it snags one weight or swimfeeder after another and refuses to release them – hence the car wheel nuts. This is not to say that this book recommends using car wheel nuts instead of lead weights, but simply to emphasize the fact that for most of the barbel fishing you will be doing you will not require a special lead. You won't need a streamlined lead for casting great distances, or an especially dumpy lead for the bolt rig, or many of the other designer leads that can be used to greater effect in carp fishing.

These two hook patterns are typical of modern hooks designed specifically for barbel (and carp) fishing.

This tackle box contains a wide selection of leads.

Barbel fishing needs no more than three types of lead: a pear-shaped bomb, a gripper lead, and an inline lead – and even that is questionable. When you cast into a river you want your bait to do one of two things: move, or remain stationary. If you want your bait to move, you use a lead that will roll; if you want it to remain stationary, you use a lead that will grip. Both of the actions required can be achieved with both types of lead simply by varying the amount of weight, but a smoother operation of the rolling action is achieved with a rounded lead; use a heavier lead for a slow roll and a lighter lead for a faster roll. A rounded inline lead will, in

theory, allow the tackle to roll along the riverbed without twisting the line as much as a rounded lead that is attached via a swivel – but that is probably truer in theory than it is in reality. A gripper lead or a flat lead will hold bottom better when you want your bait to stay where you cast it.

Most of the leads you buy today are coated in one way or another to keep them dull and to make them better able to blend in with the bottom. However, in most situations a plain lead-coloured lead will suffice. If you are fishing a particularly clear river in bright sunshine then another option is a lead that isn't really a lead

Using a safety clip is one way to achieve a rig that won't tether a barbel should the main line break.

but a real stone with a swivel inserted at one end, or bored to become an inline weight. These come in the normal various shapes and sizes that you can find on most riverbeds, and theory has it, are less likely to spook wary barbel. These stone weights are lighter for a given size than lead weights, and to hold bottom a much bigger one is required than the equivalent lead weight. But maybe they can just give you that little extra edge when fishing in very clear water, and if that gives you extra confidence, then it's got to be worth it.

If you want the bolt effect, you need a heavy lead that is semi-fixed: that is, fixed enough so that the line can't pull through it when the fish takes the bait, but free enough to be able to come clear of the tackle should you get snagged or broken by some other means. It is also an advantage for the lead to be able to slide along the line when playing a barbel that could charge in and out of dense weedbeds: by being free to slide up the line without getting caught in the weed there is less likelihood of the tackle becoming snagged. Leads can be released through the use of a safety clip, but a far better way to fish a river, especially for barbel, is with a lead whose swivel jams on to a tapered sleeve – and this set-up can easily be changed from a bolt rig to a running rig.

Sometimes additional weight is needed on the line above the main weight to pin down the line away from the rig. By doing this you go some way towards keeping the main line at this point away from barbel that are feeding in the baited area, which could become spooked should they brush against the line. One way to do this is through using a backlead that slides on the main line but is prevented from getting nearer to the main lead by a couple of float stops. Several types of lead are suitable for this; some anglers use standard carp flying backleads while others use drilled bullets.

A few small blobs of Kryston Heavy Metal is another useful product for pinning down a trace and weighting a hook for trundling meat.

Swivels and Beads

You will need swivels in sizes 8 and 10, some size 8 ring swivels and some quick-change swivels. Avoid any type of swivel with a diamond eye, as these seem prone to weakening the line. Also useful are quick-change clips, small round

This inline lead makes an excellent back lead for fast currents.

rubber beads, tapered beads, tapered sleeves, silicon sleeves and sliding float stops.

The use of hair rigs requires the paraphernalia that comes with it, so baiting needles, bait drills and hair stops are all regarded as standard barbel equipment. Korum do a useful variation on a hair stop, known as the Pellet Stop, which partially inserts into the drilled hole of the pellet but has two flat feet on which the pellet sits. By having a selection of these in different lengths it allows you to vary the length of the hair. The use of latex bait bands on a hair is another option, and a better one than banding direct to the hook. If you use braid, then a pair of braid scissors is essential, and an ordinary pair is useful, as is a diamond hook sharpener.

RIGHT: Keep all your rig bits safe and tidy in a purpose-made tackle box and it will be easy to find swivels, beads and other bits and pieces.

BELOW: A selection of useful tools for fine-tuning rigs.

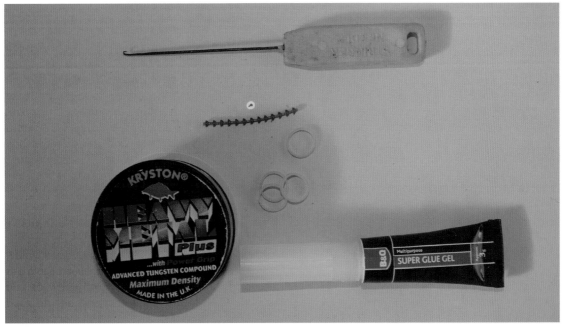

Feeding the Swim

Swimfeeders

Swimfeeder fishing requires a selection of blockend and open-end feeders in various sizes and weights. Mesh feeders are best for the open-end, groundbait feeders. They'll need to be well made and tough, for barbel fishing can be very hard on feeders. You will find it useful to have spare 'ski' leads or 'dead cow' leads, which are different names for add-on leads for feeders.

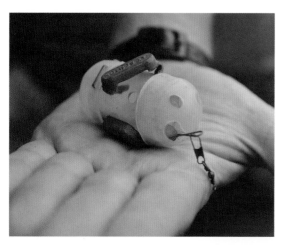

Bait Droppers

Bait droppers come in several sizes, from mini ones for delicate canal work through to standard ones for roach fishing, to large and extra-large ones that are perfect for barbel fishing. There are several designs, though they are all variations on a theme of having a container for bait with an opening lid held in place with a wire rod that is tripped when the dropper hits bottom. Whichever sort you buy, check that it works efficiently; one that opens too soon or not at all is useless. Many anglers paint bright metal droppers with a matt paint to dull the shine and avoid scaring the fish, though it is likely that the fish will quickly high tail it out of the swim during the commotion of baiting up with a dropper.

LEFT: *A robust blockend feeder complete with added weight.*

BELOW: *Barbel of this size are a worthwhile target for swimfeeder fishing.*

A big bait dropper can soon lay down a bed of hemp or other particles.

Catapults

A catapult with a pouch suitable for pellet and boilie feeding is recommended, because although most of the feed you introduce will be via a baitdropper or swimfeeder it is often a good idea to supplement this with the occasional helping of loose feed. For trotting, a good catapult or two is a must. You need one with a large pouch as you will be feeding pouchfuls of hemp and casters, or maggots or sweetcorn. It is useful to have spare elastic as there's little worse than breaking the elastic midway through a session.

PVA Bags and String

As an alternative to using hand feeding, swimfeeders and bait droppers, a PVA bag for pellets or stringer for boilies are two other means of getting bait down into the vicinity of your hookbait.

Holdalls

Rucksacks and Holdalls

There is a wide variety of rucksacks and holdalls available that will do the job for barbel fishing. It is worth remembering that the bigger the

In some situations a good catapult is useful for feeding at distance, but be careful you don't spread your feed too widely.

This is a compact and well designed carryall, but many anglers prefer rucksacks.

holdall or rucksack, the greater the temptation to fill it, and as it is advantageous to be mobile when barbel fishing you may find yourself lugging much more around than you intended. The secret, if there is one, is to take the trouble to examine what you are carrying on a regular basis and decide just how vital each item really is. Though of course, there is nothing worse than getting on the bank and finding some essential piece of kit is still at home.

As this chapter demonstrates, there is a lot of kit that you can take for barbelling, but mostly you need to have a good idea of the style of fishing that you intend to pursue on your intended venue. This means that you don't need to be prepared for absolutely every eventuality and can pare down your kit requirements to what you really need on a particular visit.

Quiver and Rod Holdalls

When it comes to carrying rods, there are several schools of thought; one is to carry a made-up rod in one hand, with the landing net in the other. Another way is to carry the rods and so on in a normal rod holdall and make up the rods when you reach your swim; and the final way is to use a purpose-made rod quiver, again with made-up rods. Also bear in mind that if you're an angler who likes to shelter under a brolly when the conditions are wet or windy, you need a holdall that can accommodate it.

For convenience, ready-made-up-rods are quick and easy, providing you are careful that the line does not get damaged when the quiver is loaded into and out of the car and during transit to the swim, which could be through thorny bushes and the like, all of which are not kind to lines. It also pays to periodically cut off a few yards of the main line and retie it to the connecting swivel. It should go without saying that regular inspection of the hook and hook-length is essential. And don't fall into the trap of always using the same rig regardless of conditions, simply because that's the one set up on the rod!

A rod quiver makes it easy to carry two or three made-up rods.

Other Gear

Rod Rests

On smaller rivers, with the rod kept low, standard extending banksticks with a screw-in rod-rest head should be suitable. On much bigger rivers you may need to keep your rods set much higher and therefore extending banksticks are required. Some barbel anglers use a sea fisherman's type tripod set-up; in fact Korum manufacture one especially for big river anglers. Rod-rest heads with one side higher than the other are recommended, the high side preventing the rod from being dislodged when the barbel bites, and the low side giving the angler more freedom to lift the rod. John Roberts make them in a fluorescent-type material, invaluable when night fishing and for preventing leaving them behind when packing up! A useful device on rivers with very high steep banks is a safety rope with a screw-in spike that you can use to get back up the bank and for extra safety when fishing a slippery bank.

Chairs

As much of barbel fishing is about sitting and waiting, you will need a comfortable chair. There are many good chairs to chose from, though many fail to make the grade because they are simply too heavy. It's rare to find barbel fishing that only involves short walks, so a truly lightweight chair is a godsend. Different rivers demand different qualities in a chair. The flat banks of the Hampshire Avon mean that you can largely dispense with the necessity of having adjustable legs, which can cut down the weight considerably; yet on many rivers, the banks are much steeper, and without adjustable legs your seat will be useless.

A different consideration is how strong a chair you need; Mark keeps trim and can get away with a lightweight chair, but some chairs are not strong enough to survive someone who weighs 17 or 18 stone or more. Some chairs are easier to carry than others; check out the chair in the tackle shop before you buy. How heavy is it? How easy is it to adjust the legs to fit sloping river banks? How strong is it? How easy is it to carry?

Betalights

Because most barbel fishing is done with the rod tip as the bite indicator, you need to be able to see the tip when it goes dark, so a betalight is an essential item of kit. This is an artificial light source powered by the radioactive

This simple rod rest is made from luminous plastic so that it's easier to see at night. The high side goes some way to preventing the rod from being dragged off it, but the low side makes it easy to strike.

The adjustable legs on this chair make easy work of the sloping banks commonly found beside many rivers.

LEFT: *A simple fitting is used to attach a betalight to the rod tip to make it easier to see bites at night.*

BELOW: *Good quality polarized sunglasses and a hat with a brim make fish spotting much easier.*

decay of tritium (H3) gas. For fishing purposes this is a small round or square glass container, slightly variable but about 15 × 2.5 mm, the inside walls of which are coated with a phosphor. As the tritium decays, it emits beta particles (high energy electrons). These electrons stimulate the phosphor, causing it to glow.

Betalights are available in several colours, but green is the common one and the most easily seen. They last for about ten to fifteen years, and fasten to the rod via a clip and silicon tube. They are bright enough to be seen in darkness, but not too bright to be obtrusive on your night vision.

Clothes for Barbel Fishing

Some dedicated barbel anglers are often distinguishable by their fishing clothes, in that they have a distinct leaning towards floppy, full-brimmed hats and Barbour waxed jackets, which fit in very nicely with their cane rods and centrepin reels. If that's what you like, then go for it! But for most of us the usual modern, breathable and waterproof clothing does us very nicely, likewise a good pair of waterproof walking boots over thick socks, unless it is your intention to wade into the river for a trotting session on the float. Weatherproof camouflage clothing has found its way into the barbel fisher's wardrobe as well as the carp fisher's – and why not, it's better than light and bright clothing that could scare every fish in the vicinity, especially when stalking on a clear river. Even in the warmer months of the year it can still get cold, and after dusk it is likely to be damp too, so don't fall into the trap of thinking the short-sleeved T-shirt that was comfortable during the day will do for that hour or so you may fish into darkness. Go prepared, and never take the English weather for granted!

A hat that has some form of brim, whether it is a 'floppy' hat or baseball cap, will shield your eyes from some of the glare. Even more useful, and vital when stalking and fish spotting, is a good pair of polarized sunglasses.

The upper Trent in full flood; you might need to wade just to get to the river bank when it's this high, though always put personal safety first.

7 BITE DETECTION AND PLAYING BARBEL

Bite Detection

Rod Top Bite Detection

There is no question that most of the time bite detection where barbel are concerned is a case of if you don't see the bite, then you're nowhere near your rod! Most barbel bites go from that gentle nodding caused by the current, to a full bend in the rod right down to the butt before you've even registered that anything has happened. Barbel bites are usually fast, vicious, aggressive pulls on the rod that don't stop until the reel's spool is spinning madly, or the rod is plunging into the river, or the angler lifts the rod and gives line. Quivertips are rarely necessary, because in the time it takes to bend a quivertip the barbel is already bending the rod. Yet it is wise to realize that although the above description of a barbel bite is true for most of the time, there are occasions, rare though they may be, when barbel are quite capable of giving a delicate bite.

Nonetheless, there are two arguments to this: one is that if you always wait for the big rod-bending bite and ignore any smaller indications, you won't hook as many fish as you might by not ignoring them and striking. The other is that if you strike at all the indications you see when barbel fishing, it can also cost you fish, because every time you miss a minor bite you are reducing the chances of that bite developing into the big one because you've spooked the fish.

Both are unquestionably valid arguments, but as always the truth of the matter lies somewhere between the two. This is where experience enters the equation, for the angler who has

Eels can be a nuisance when using halibut pellets or other meaty/fishy baits.

Graham keeps low while touch legering on the Dane.

ample experience of both types of bite has a much better chance of knowing if he should strike at a minor bite, or leave it to develop into a major one.

If in any doubt, the best advice, at least when barbel fishing, is to leave it and wait for the big one.

Most barbel anglers are quite paranoid about pinning the main line to the bottom, using lead core, back leads and anything else they can get their hands on to ensure the line is out of the way of the barbel as it roots for food in the vicinity of the hookbait. They believe that when a barbel touches the line it frightens it out of the swim, or at least puts it on high alert to danger. It is debatable, however, just how much touching the line affects the barbel; but most anglers follow the doctrine of pinning the line to the bottom 'just in case' – which, incidentally, is why we do many things that are more a matter of opinion than a matter of fact. Granted, barbel in clear water have been seen to shy away from main line that isn't pinned down out of the way.

But ask a bunch of experienced barbel anglers what they have seen barbel shy away from, and there are not many items of tackle and varieties of bait that are not mentioned.

Many, if not most, barbel anglers have no knowledge of the reasons behind pinning the line, and many who are indeed aware of it have no qualms at all about leaving the main line open to being fouled. Some actually set up to ensure that the barbel *does* touch the line as much as possible, and use the false indications as a warning of the real bite that usually follows. They often use a quivertip with the express purpose of exaggerating the pre-knocks, the false bites, and it is a fact that many of the anglers who use 'the knock', as it's called, are very successful indeed. In a deeper, murkier spate river, it's questionable whether the barbel would know the difference between brushing against a line and brushing against a strand of weed. These authors offer 'fishing the knock' as an alternative to the more popular 'pin the line' approach. Try both and see for yourself.

Touch Legering

At the other extreme of possible barbel bites are those that make hardly any movement on the rod tip or quivertip, and the best way of detecting these is to touch leger, which is to feel for bites through the line. Make no mistake though, touch legering is not always the best way of detecting bites, no matter how feeble they are, but in some circumstances it can be the only way, not only of detecting them, but of providing the information you need in order to know how to deal with them. As well as knowing *how* to touch leger, the trick is to know *when* to touch leger.

Forget about those cynical anglers who try to run down the method because they haven't taken the trouble to learn it – those who say, 'Touch legering is no good when it's freezing and your fingers are numb', and 'You don't need to touch leger when the barbel are ripping the rod out of your hands.' This is not because what they say isn't true, but because it's obvious that touch legering is no good then, and you use something more appropriate! Do you need to be told that you don't prop up the rod and watch for bites on the rod tip of an Avon-type rod when fishing for gudgeon? Or constantly reminded that there is no point in sitting alert and holding the rod and line, feeling for bites, when you're out all night and expecting only one or two bites from the occasional big fish? Of course you don't, it's obvious. And the right time to touch leger is just as obvious to an experienced exponent of the art.

So What is Touch Legering?

Touch legering is usually described as feeling for bites, but that isn't by any means the full picture: it's more accurate to say that touch legering is feeling and analysing bites. The detection of the bite in the first instance (feeling for it) is only part of the process; the next part is far more important – actually feeling the bite and understanding what is going on. Put more simply, touch legering can be used to detect bites, but it is no more efficient than detecting them with some kind of mechanical indicator or even the rod top: it's what happens after detecting the bite that touch legering comes into its own, when the bite is still going on and your fingers are interpreting all the signals.

Don't make the mistake of thinking that all

Using a quivertip to register bites, Graham keeps well back from the edge of the bank on the River Mease.

Comfortable and relaxing – touch legering the easy way.

barbel bites are those aggressive pulls that bend the rod down to the butt. There are times when barbel can be quite subtle when they bite, and unless you have actually seen them doing this in clear water, the only way you would know you had a bite was if you were holding the line and could feel it. Think of this: if someone strokes a guitar string at one end very lightly you would be unlikely to see the movement at the other end. But if you were touching that string with a fingertip ...

Touch legering can therefore be summarized in one sentence: detecting and analysing bites through the sense of touch. Of course we know as well as any experienced barbel angler that you don't often need to touch leger, but if you *do* know how to do it properly, you then have the choice between feeling for and analysing bites, or leaving those slight trembles you see on the rod top and hoping that big bite develops.

The Mechanics of Touch Legering
There is no single exact way to touch leger. Most anglers allow a loop of line between butt ring and reel to lie across the pad of the index finger of the hand that turns the reel; others allow the line to lie over two or more fingers of

that hand. Yet others have the line coming up from the reel and hooked over the index finger of the hand that holds the rod. Graham's personal preference is to have the line lying across the middle and index finger of his reel hand, with the emphasis on his middle finger; when he's feeling a bite he occasionally wiggles those two fingers very, very slightly so the pressure is transferred from one to the other, because for some reason it heightens his sense of touch. More than anything, touch legering will teach you which of your fingers is the most receptive to touch.

Let us also put to rest another long-founded assumption: you don't have to point the rod at the end tackle to touch leger. Cutting out all the angles so that the line has minimum friction through the rings, especially the tip ring, is a good thing to do if you are relying totally on feeling the bites. However, you can often touch leger in combination with a quivertip or a soft rod top so there is some visual indication to go by as well as tactile indication. Very often this combination of visual and tactile bite analysis is the best of all, because then you have two elements transmitting information. It's true that the friction of the line through the tip ring and down the rod will reduce the strength of the tactile signal, but you have to remember that touch legering is not always about detecting ultra-sensitive bites, but more about analysing and knowing how to deal with more robust bites. Thinking that touch legering is only for detecting ultra-sensitive bites is a mistake made by too many anglers.

How you sit and hold the rod is very important when touch legering. Being comfortable is important to any type of fishing, but when touch legering it is essential or you will not be able to concentrate sufficiently on what you're doing. One way is to sit with the rod in your right hand with your forearm resting along your thigh. The rod is at an angle of about 45 degrees to the bank and laid on a rod rest at a point about two thirds the length of the rod from butt. The moment you see any sign of a bite (unless it's a self-hooker) you lift the rod out of the rest, and as you move the rod a few inches towards the fish you take up the slack line by drawing off a loop of line between butt ring and reel, which

becomes the loop that lies across your index finger and middle finger.

You then concentrate on watching the quivertip or rod tip and feeling the line. Most often bites are both seen and felt at the same time, but depending on what you feel, you either strike, offer the fish some slack, or just keep in touch and feel what is going on. Occasionally give the line one or two sharp pulls. The strength of the bite, or lack of tension if the fish has moved towards you, may be steady or it may be erratic – more of a jabbing sensation. It may feel like a vibration. According to what you feel (and see) dictates your reaction. It is difficult to describe adequately the different sensations you will feel in your fingertips if you have no experience of touch legering: it's something you will have to do a number of times in order to gain the experience that will make touch legering meaningful. But don't let that put you off, because you will come to realize that it's been worth it in the end.

Who needs touch legering for barbel? We all do, although not very often, but on those very

The specialized nature of a barbel's mouth and its barbules.

rare occasions when they decide to flick their barbules over the line as they mouth the bait, giving a bite that feels as if a hacksaw blade is being drawn across the line, you'll be glad you knew how to touch leger, and knew what such a bite felt like.

Playing Barbel

Pound for pound the barbel is one of the hardest fighting fish in British waters. Couple that with the fact that they are often fighting in a powerful current, and you can safely say you have a battle on your hands when you hook one. They fight from the moment they pick up the bait and turn downstream with it, accelerating away at great speed, to when they slide over the frame of the landing net.

Unless the fish you hook is heading for a snag (discussed in the next section) then let it go, but don't let it have things all its own way by allowing it to take line easily: make it work for every inch of line it takes from you – make it pay for every inch in units of energy, and at every chance you can, take every inch back. Show it who's boss, but in a way that is controlled and

patient, but uncompromising. It's better for both you and the fish to land it as quickly as possible: the longer it takes, the more likelihood there is of it shedding the hook, or shredding the line, and the greater is the risk of it becoming too exhausted to make a quick recovery.

Use the rod, not the reel, to play barbel: this may seem an obvious piece of advice, yet too many anglers, when battling with hard-fighting fish, allow the rod to point towards the fish and try to control it by applying more or less pressure via the reel's drag function. That is not a good way to play fish! View the reel as no more than a safety feature, a device that retrieves line and has a failsafe function, the drag that kicks in when there is nothing more you can do with the rod. To understand how to use a rod to play a fish, take a deeper, closer look at a rod and relate its design to how best to use it to play a fish. Picture a rod as a shock absorber in three sections: the tip section, the middle section and the butt section. The tip section is the easiest to bend; the middle section still bends but needs far more pressure; and finally the butt section can still bend but needs a great amount of pressure to do so, and the bend in it is negligible.

If we want to apply a little pressure on the fish we bend the tip section into it. To apply more pressure, we change the angle of the rod so that the tip points more towards the fish, and apply pressure from the middle section. If we want to apply ultimate pressure, we change the angle to point almost directly at the rod, and apply pressure with the butt section. Never point the rod directly at the fish because then the rod has no function whatsoever, resulting in the fish being in direct contact with the reel.

Playing a fish now becomes a sequence of movements with the rod to counteract the movements of the fish and the speed with which those movements are made, with the reel's drag kicking in when the pressure from the fish almost matches the breaking strain of the line. 'Feel' the rod and make it an extension of your arm. Put your reactions on high alert so that you are prepared for sudden and unexpected dashes for freedom from the fish – and never, ever, assume that the fish is beaten and relax those reactions. Don't allow the fish to accelerate, to build up speed. The further it can run unchecked, the more speed it can build, to a point where the momentum can build beyond the power of the rod and the strength of the line to stop it. As was advised at the start of this section – *make the fish work hard for every inch of line it takes!*

Changing Position

Sometimes when fishing adjacent to thick weedbeds such as those found on our clearer rivers such as the Hampshire Avon, it pays to change position when a hooked barbel has managed to dive into the weed. Rather than trying to bully the fish from the optimum position you've chosen to cast from, move to a position that is downstream of the weed. Just keep a tight line

The thick streamer weed on the Hampshire Avon means you need to get downstream of hooked barbel to make it easier to pull them out of it.

This swim has plenty of snags.

on the barbel while you carefully make your way to a predefined spot, where you've left your landing net. This offers two advantages: you then have the current working for you, and you'll be pulling the fish in the same direction the weed is leaning towards; and it can be pulled out much more easily than trying to pull it 'against the grain' of the weedbed.

Snag Fishing

The key to successful snag fishing is balanced tackle, as described in the section above, but with the whole kit stepped up somewhat: the rod a half pound heavier in test curve, the line a couple of pounds heavier in breaking strain, and the hook at least one size bigger and, more important, in a heavier gauge wire. The final ingredient to snag fishing is an overdose of confidence. But as well as having to balance the tackle you use, you also need some well balanced reasons for snag fishing in the first place. Of course, the simple answer is that you want to snag fish because the fish are there, they have succumbed to the never-ending angling pressure found in open water, and at least most of the time hide away in a safe haven, usually a

labyrinth of tree roots or branches, or thick weed – they tend to feed in, or very close to, this area with much more confidence than they do elsewhere.

However, you should at least try to entice the fish away from the snags with some judicious feeding before attempting to manhandle them out with snag tackle. And if you think that trying to extract fish from snags, or prevent fish from entering nearby snags, will damage them in any way at all, then don't do it. Only you can be the judge of that when you consider the situation that's facing you. Graham has done a lot of snag fishing and he can honestly say that it hasn't harmed the fish at all. It's mainly a matter of using the right tackle, and especially a heavy gauge hook, and with 100 per cent confidence in what you're doing.

The bottom line is this: to extract fish from snags, or prevent them from getting into nearby snags, you have to use strong tackle. That's about as basic as you can get, but there are anglers who think they can snag fish effectively with too light gear through fancy rod work. How often have you heard someone say, 'Just pull them towards the snag and they'll swim away from it.' Well, that may be acceptable in some situations for some species, but here we're talking about barbel of 8lb or more, and strong rods, heavy line and tough hooks are the starting point and there should be no compromise.

Balanced Tackle
Too many anglers don't use the right union between rod and line. The rule of thumb is simple: match the rod and line so that the rod can bend to its full potential, but not to the point where it locks solid. That's the first thing to get right; the second is to make sure you use a heavy gauge hook. There is no point marrying the rod and line together and then using a hook that will either bend or break under the pressure you need to apply. Furthermore, fine wire hooks have no place in snag fishing due to the potential damage they can cause to the fish's mouth due to the cheese-cutter effect.

The tackle need not be as strong as many anglers imagine, for the simple reason that too many anglers don't use their tackle to its full potential. That's all right when you can afford to take your time and enjoy the fight (within reason, but not to the point of exhausting the fish), and where there are no snags to contend with. But it makes no sense at all to play around with 2lb TC rods and 12lb line when the fish is heading for a snag or a neighbour's swim, when all that's needed is to bend the rod properly into the fish to stop it and turn it.

At some time or other you must have been snagged, and had to pull to either free the line or break it. And when you've been using 10lb or heavier line there must have been times when

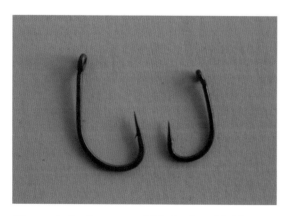

Heavy wire hooks are essential for hook-and-hold barbel fishing.

A Word of Caution

When pulling for a break, don't do it by bending the rod into it. Put the rod in the rest and release some line, wrap the line around a bankstick or similar (line will cut into your hands), and pull at it from behind a tree or some other cover that will give you protection, for if that tackle should suddenly pull free it could fly at you like a bullet and cause very serious injury, or worse. Also keep an eye out for passers-by during the whole procedure.

you've really struggled to break it, even with a direct pull with the line wrapped around a bankstick. You've pointed the rod at the snag, or wrapped the line around something solid, and pulled – you've actually felt the line stretch, and couldn't believe it when it didn't break until you pulled far more than you would have thought possible. Breaking well tied 12lb or heavier line takes some doing, and often involves taking several backward steps in order to succeed, especially when using mono that has a certain amount of stretch.

Technique
Some consider snag fishing as tantamount to pulling the fish's head off, so how can something so raw and brutal be described as a technique? This is where most would-be snag fishers make their mistake, because they think it *is* just a crude heaving exercise between man and fish, with more luck than judgement ruling the day. Of course a lot of heaving *is* involved, and, like many aspects of fishing, there is some luck involved, too.

The first thing to get right is your mindset. When you hook a big fish in or close to a snag, it must be firmly planted in your mind that you are going to bend that rod to a point where it may never have been before. You are going to feel the cork bend and creak under your fingers, and you are going to see that rod take on a curve that you never thought was possible. Keep those times when you have had to pull for a

Ready for action in a confined and snaggy swim.

break firmly in mind: remember them well the next time you go snag fishing, because they will help you to break through that psychological barrier that sets good snag fishers apart from the rest.

The second important point to remember is that you do *not* sit back from the rod. You sit right by the rod, preferably with your hand on it (and you never fish more than one rod when snag fishing) but at least with the handle within easy reach and the reel's drag tightened down. As the fish picks up the bait it immediately realizes it's made a mistake and heads off for the thick of the snag. You should be ready to counter that run before it can develop into a fast run and therefore a greater force to counter. The idea is to pile the pressure on the fish before it can develop the speed and acceleration it needs to dig in. It is the simple formula that says speed is equal to the distance moved/time taken, and force is equal to mass multiplied by acceleration that is so significant. Where snag

fishing is concerned it says, 'Don't allow the fish any time to move any distance in order to develop sufficient speed to build enough momentum to beat you!'

What should happen is this: the rod bends over as the fish takes the bait and immediately dives for the snag, so you lift the rod and bend it some more – really bend it. The fish will try to bend it even more, and at this point you may start to panic – but you push that out of your mind, hold your breath, and think of the last time you tried to pull for a break, and then bend the rod even more. Don't give an inch, other than what the bend in the rod will allow. The barbel will keep trying to dig deeper into the snag and more often than not you'll end up with a stalemate, where the fish can't dig any deeper, and you can't reasonably pull any harder. Many times the fish will come away from the snag much more easily than you imagined and in no time at all you're playing it a few yards from the snag but in open water.

So you breathe a sigh of relief and ease off the pressure, maybe even slacken off the drag a notch or two. But that's the *worst* thing you can do at this stage, for that just gives the fish the freedom and space it needs to wind up enough acceleration to dive back into the snag. It's hard to ignore that feeling of relief when the fish is clear of the snag and apparently not fighting quite so desperately, but whatever you do, keep that bend in the rod and get the fish well away from the snag before you begin to ease off at all. And even then be very wary of them making a sudden and determined attempt to have another go. Many a big barbel has been lost (before the lesson was learnt) through thinking too soon that it was beaten.

Snag fishing can be awesome, heart-pounding fishing. But that's the only way to tackle snag fishing: with the right tackle and the confidence to use it to full effect. You have to go for it, and go for it with a vengeance.

LEFT: *This weedy Throop, Dorset Stour swim has a mixture of thick weed, pipe reeds and barbel. There's no room for manoeuvre, just confident strong-arm playing tactics.*

BELOW: *Graham piles on the pressure in a snaggy swim.*

8 STANDARD RIGS AND METHODS

Legering

Why leger? Fishing with a legered bait is by far the most popular means to fish for barbel, as indeed it is for most of our bigger, hard-fighting species. This is not an indication that suggests float fishing is an unfeasible way to catch barbel, but a sure sign that the opportunity to float fish and the desire to float fish are wanting where specialist anglers are concerned. A great deal of barbel fishing is done from a little before dusk and into the night, and the brutal truth, too, is that barbel anglers in particular just don't know how to float fish for the species (that, however,

can be remedied by reading the float fishing chapter in this book).

Nevertheless, it is still a fact that the majority of barbel anglers will leger fish for the very simple reason that it is the method that best lends itself to catching them, for the majority of barbel swims are not suitable for float fishing. Much of the time the species wants a stationary bait, or a moving bait that is best presented with leger tackle, and very often night time is when the barbel feed best. Legering, without doubt, is also a method that is much easier to master than float fishing.

Legering is seen as the method to pin a bait to

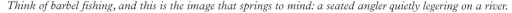

Think of barbel fishing, and this is the image that springs to mind: a seated angler quietly legering on a river.

the bottom, where the fish are fed in that spot and encouraged to move to the hookbait. But there is much more to legering than that, as you will see when you read through this chapter.

Balanced Tackle of the Right Strength

Whatever method we choose it is important to use balanced tackle. Balanced tackle means creating a tackle set-up where each component – from rods, reels, lines, right through to the hook – is ideally matched to the other components. When the set-up is right there are very few weak links, and each part of the set-up is able to perform to its best.

The most important thing to bear in mind when deciding on tackle strength is that you don't get any more credit for landing barbel on light tackle, and there is no point in making it more difficult than you have to by fishing unnecessarily light. All light tackle achieves is a greater possibility of a lost fish, a swim that

is disturbed for longer than necessary, and a fish that has been played to exhaustion. Tackle should always be built from the weakest link, and the weakest link should always be the hook length, so that if you suffer a breakage for any reason it will most likely be just the hook and a short length of line that you lose. And, most important, it will only be the hook and a short length of line left in the fish's mouth.

So the first thing to decide is how strong a hook link you need to safely land barbel from the swim you're fishing. A 6lb hook length is about as light as you're ever going to need, and this for smaller shoal barbel up to about 5lb when you're trying to catch them from open, snag-free water. Even then you will probably get away with 8lb line. The most common hook length strength for barbel bigger than 6lb is 10lb bs, and 12lb is the usual choice for those anglers who fish for big barbel that reach double figures where snags are not too far away. In rare

These overhanging bushes give cover to barbel, but also restrict your ability to follow a hooked fish downstream.

This simple feeder rig (shown here without silicon sleeves) is ideal for big river barbelling.

instances, barbel anglers will use 15lb hook lengths when fishing for really big barbel that are feeding very close to snags.

Once you've decided on hook length strength you'll know what strength of main line to use, which should be about 2lb bs stronger. Then choose a reel that will handle comfortably this diameter and strength of line, and a rod that can play hard-fighting barbel on that strength of line. A rod that is too light for the line won't be able to deal properly with the fish, which will then be free to dictate the fight. On the other hand, a rod that is too heavy will not provide the essential shock absorber effect and therefore there will be a greater risk of the line breaking when the fish makes a sudden lunge. Another danger of using a rod that is too heavy is there is more chance of the hook hold failing.

Legering Techniques

The standard way to leger for barbel on many rivers is to cast downstream and away from the bank. This technique works well enough most of the time and helps the bolt effect of the rig, because usually barbel take off downstream at a great rate of knots when they feel the hook, and hook themselves against the rod. Its main disadvantage is that when you hook a downstream barbel you will have to bring it back upriver against the flow, and if the swim is weedy,

against the weed. Pulling a barbel into weed in this way is far from ideal, so there are times when it makes sense for you to get smartly downstream of your fishing position to be in a position to pull the fish the same way the weed is leaning, rather than against it. Sometimes this isn't feasible if there are trees and bushes between swims that are too big to pass your rod around.

The alternative is to fish upstream, which is a very different technique; it is covered in Chapter 9.

Basics Rigs

When it comes to legering for barbel there are two main, basic rigs; one is nothing more than a weight, either attached to the line (fixed) or sliding freely on the line (running); the other is exactly the same, but with a swimfeeder instead of a weight. The variation comes from the modifications that we can build around these two methods. The deviations from the basic rig include the type of weight, the method of attaching the weight, the size of weight, the hook link, the hook, the use of back leads, and the type and size of swimfeeder and its means of attachment, of which more later in this chapter.

Unlike carp, which appear to be a more intelligent fish, barbel usually feed in a very simple way, and more often than not a simple rig will be enough to present a bait in such a way that the fish will take the bait and be hooked efficiently. The difference between carp and barbel, and the reason why simpler rigs are sufficient for barbel, is that carp will often suck and blow at a bait, taking it into their mouth and blowing it out, tasting it, and generally inspecting it to see if it's safe. Barbel are much more inclined to forego any preliminaries and mouth a bait straight off the bottom. This means that most of the time a hair rig isn't needed to aid presentation, although with most baits it is still an advantage to have a hook that is not impeded by being buried, or partially buried, in a bait.

Each of these methods has its advantages and disadvantages. Straightforward legering without a swimfeeder is usually the best method when the number of barbel present in a swim is small. This enables you to use other methods of feeding the swim to control the rate of feed into it without the encumbrance of a swimfeeder. It is a method ideally suited for targeting big barbel where you must do as much as possible to avoid alerting them of your presence, in which case the regular casting of a swimfeeder is likely to be detrimental. This approach is much more 'bait and wait'.

On the other hand, the regular casting, constant feeding approach that fishing a feeder entails is well suited to swims with a good head

Standard weights such as these, a flattened bomb and a grip lead, in various sizes, will cope with the majority of barbel fishing situations.

of shoal barbel; even the actual splash of the feeder hitting the water can be like a dinner gong when the fish are hungry and there are plenty of them to incite competition for the food. Even bigger barbel will respond to the splash of a swimfeeder when they're hungry enough to put their fear to one side.

Whichever rig you use, the simpler it is the better – the more beads, swivels and other paraphernalia you use to construct it, the more likely it is to tangle or snag. That doesn't mean that we must not use any swivels or beads, but only that each component of the rigs we devise should have a practical purpose that adds to the efficiency of the rig and not be there for mere decoration. It is all too easy to devise complex rigs that in reality do nothing to make the rig work better, and in some instances actually hinder the efficiency of its operation.

Before we describe some of the basic legering rigs for barbel, let's take a closer look at the most common component parts.

Leads and Other Weights

Leads and other weights come in many shapes and sizes. Traditionally, anglers have used lead to make weights for several reasons: it is a cheap, very dense metal that has a low melting point and is easy to cast into different shapes using a mould. The law banning weights of less than an ounce being made from lead means that 'leads' under 1oz will probably be made from zinc or brass. It is still customary, however, to refer to angling weights of any size as leads, even though they may not be made from that material.

Most of the weights, lead or otherwise these days, have been coated with some kind of material to make them blend in with the river bed. The coatings vary from plain weed green, through sand, silt and gravel colours, to rough coatings that look like algae-covered pebbles. And then we have Stonze weights that are real stones just like those found on the bed of most rivers. Stones don't have the density of lead weights, and you need a much bigger stone than you would a lead to hold bottom. Their advantage, however, is that they are totally natural and possibly the best thing to use in low, clear rivers. They are also much better for the environment when lost.

RIGHT: Natural Stonze weights may help in low clear water, but denser lead weights are more practical in heavier flows.

BELOW: In very strong currents a grip lead holds better than a smooth weight.

Lead Shapes

The most common lead used is the pear-shaped bomb, at least in stillwater, but river anglers have come to realize that unless they want to roll a bait through the swim, a lead with a better grip makes more sense. Pear-shaped bombs can be flattened with a hammer to give them better grip, but it is more common these days for barbel anglers to use commercially available square leads or gripper leads, which are the carp angler's pear-shaped version of the sea angler's watch leads.

These leads have swivels or wire loops fitted, through which the line is threaded; but there are other leads, known as 'in-lines', where the line is threaded through the body of the lead – so nothing new there, as 'bullet' leads have been around for several decades. Today, although the bullet is still around and still has its uses, the modern in-line lead is more elongated and streamlined.

What Size of Lead?

We base the size of lead we choose on several considerations, the main one being how important it is for the lead to hold position. If we want the lead to roll through a swim and at a certain rate, then we need to be much fussier when choosing the actual weight (for more about this, *see* Chapter 9 when upstream legering and

rolling baits are discussed). Most of the time we want to cast a bait to a certain spot in the swim, and for the lead to hold the bait in that spot until a fish takes it – there is no point discovering a hotspot in a swim, only for the current or the slightest bit of debris coming down the current to dislodge the lead and carry the bait to a barren area. The bait should be pinned down quite firmly, and therefore a lead should be chosen that is comfortably heavy enough, especially at times of flood or in autumn when fallen leaves and other debris are waterborne, to hold position.

Also, consider if you are going to attach PVA bags of feed, and the fact that very often the PVA bag will make it more difficult for the lead

PVA bags of feed such as pellets are a practical way to feed a swim accurately.

could be the answer to get them to accept a bait. A mono that is thinner in diameter for a given strength, and more supple, offering better bait presentation, is co-polymer, but you have to be very careful with it as it is also a much more delicate material. Co-polymer monos are not recommended unless you are fishing in open water with no sharp objects of any description.

Another reason for not using an ordinary mono is if you want your hook length to lie flat on the bottom, and this is where fluorocarbon mono comes in, because this material, as well as being more invisible in water, is denser and lies flatter. Some anglers claim that fluoro is more prone to nicks, cuts and abrasions than ordinary mono, but both authors have found that this is not necessarily true if you use a top quality fluoro, such as Kryston's Incognito. A fluoro-coated mono (ordinary mono with a top layer of fluorocarbon) is, in theory at least, somewhere between the two.

The best presentation is probably via a soft braid, but soft braids usually mean having to use some kind of tubing above the lead or feeder to avoid tangles when casting as they are prone to wrapping round the main line when in flight. There is nothing wrong with using a rig tube to avoid tangles, but it's another component best left off the rig unless absolutely necessary.

One way round it is to use a coated braid, such as Kryston's Mantis, which is available in

to grip for those few seconds before the PVA dissolves and releases the feed. Always make sure the lead is heavy enough to grip bottom while the feed is dispensed.

Hook Links

Hook-Link Material

There are several choices for hook-link material, the most common being regular monofilament. There are plenty of good, tough monos that are reliable and most of the time will catch barbel, but on those days when barbel are particularly wary or not really hungry, something different

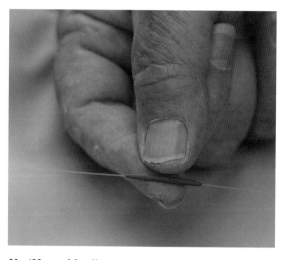

Use 'Heavy Metal' tungsten putty to pin down hook links.

Hook pulls are rare due to the tough mouth of a barbel, seen here on a fine lower Severn fish.

various colours to suit the river bed you're fishing over. Coated braids are stiff enough to avoid tangles, yet the skin can be stripped back for an inch or two from the hook, leaving a supple section where it matters. Coated braids are also good for fishing close to snags, because the skin over the braid makes the line less prone to abrasion.

Any hook link can be made to lie flat on the bottom with the application of a few tiny blobs of Heavy Metal tungsten putty.

Hook-Link Length
Although thousands of barbel have been caught on short 6in to 9in hook links – and even shorter when using the Method feeder – the current thinking is that 2ft and even longer hook links are better. There are, of course, advantages and disadvantages with both, and the recommendation is that you shouldn't jump into one camp or the other, but should experiment with both long and short hook links when the barbel are playing hard to hook, or coming off the hook when playing them. It must be said, though, that the barbel is a species that bites so aggressively a hook pull is rare.

Longer hook links are currently in favour due to the fact that the bait lies further away from the main line and therefore the chances of the barbel fouling it and producing 'line bites' are shortened. Also, if particularly wary barbel in clear rivers are spooked by the sight of leads and swimfeeders, and any other components of a rig, there is less chance of this happening if the bait lies further away from those components.

There is also the theory that a longer hook link gives the barbel a better chance to take the bait without feeling the resistance of the lead. This is, of course, debatable, as it much depends in which direction the barbel mouths the bait – directly downstream, which is the usual way, and they will feel the lead, feeder or rod tip however long the hook link is. If they mouth the bait upwards, or back towards the lead or feeder, in theory they may not feel much. The reality, however, is that most often they drop down on to a bait, mouth it, and then turn downstream, and that they would feel enough to cause them to bolt downstream if they mouthed the bait and moved in any other direction. Longer hook links probably appear to work better for the main reason that they place the bait further from leads, feeder and the main line.

Hair Rigs and Bait Bands

The original purpose of the hair rig was to present a bait that would act naturally when being investigated by carp, but it was soon realized that its greatest asset is that it leaves the hook free to do its job. Prior to the development of the hair rig the only way to attach a bait to the hook was to pass the hook through it, which is fine for many 'soft' baits, including common barbel baits such as maggots, casters, worms, sweetcorn and luncheon meat. But where 'hard' baits are concerned, hooking the bait by passing the hook through it is not only difficult, but results in many lost fish due to the hook being impeded and causing poor penetration. Nowadays most barbel baits are hair rigged, or the bait is attached to the hook with a silicon rubber

band. Perhaps only worms, soft pellets and sweetcorn, and small baits such as maggot and caster, are still hooked directly.

The subject of the hair length is much discussed in carp and barbel fishing circles. Just how close should the bait be to the bend of the hook? And as always there is diverse opinion, at one extreme the school that says the bait should be touching the hook, and at the other those who say it should be at least half an inch away from the hook. Where carp are concerned, the thinking on all of this is constantly changing, but it is generally accepted by most experienced barbel anglers that a short hair is all that is needed for barbel; in fact if it wasn't for the unimpeded bait factor there would be no need at all to hair rig when barbel fishing, simply because barbel feed by mouthing a bait, with little of the sucking and blowing associated with carp. It is therefore recommended that the hair length should be long enough for the bait not to be tight to the hook, but not so long that it can swing round and mask the point of the hook.

The first experiments in developing the hair rig were with human hair, which explains how it got its name. And then in the early days, as hair rigging evolved, 'hairs' were made with very fine monofilament or braid, as fine as 1lb bs, and quite separate from the knot that tied the hook to the hook link. The advent of the knotless

It is a simple operation to thread a boilie on to a hair using a baiting needle.

knot, however, where the hair is part of the knot that attaches the hook, has simplified the way anglers tie a hair rig, and it is well proven by now that the hair does not have to be fine and supple, confirming that the main asset of the hair rig is that it leaves the hook unencumbered.

In a barbel fishing situation where there are both barbel and chub present, one observation worth noting is that it is possible to lessen the chance of hooking chub by lengthening the hair. Chub are notoriously hard to hook on hair rigs due to their habit of picking up a bait and moving off with it still held in their lips. Chub anglers wanting to hook chub with hair-rigged baits generally use a very short hair so that the bait is touching the bend of the hook. So when a barbel angler wants to avoid hooking chub, so as not to disturb the swim unnecessarily by catching an unwanted species, one way is to increase the length of the hair so that the chub are less likely to get hooked. It won't stop the chub picking up the bait, even dislodging the lead at times, but at least the swim will remain undisturbed by a played fish.

A variation of the hair rig is to tie a bait band to the end of the hair (*see* picture), and then it is a simple process to attach pellets simply by slipping them into the bait band. It is even easier with the aid of a bait bander.

A point to remember is that if you intend to leave a hook bait in the water for a prolonged period it is better to use the standard hair rig and hair stop method, because a partially dissolved pellet can slip out of the band.

Back Leads

To reduce line bites, especially when fishing at close range, many barbel anglers use a flying back lead. Thread it on the main line – a drilled bullet is commonly used – and stop it at least three feet from the main lead with a couple of float stops. This will pin down the line for some distance back from the rig. This back lead also helps get the main line away from drifting pieces of weed and other debris, such as leaves following the autumn fall and the crud that always comes with floodwater. When fishing with a back lead, or at any time when debris is coming down with the current, always release several yards of line after casting so that the line has

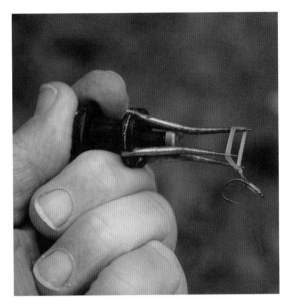

A bait bander tool makes it easy to insert pellets into a bait band.

more chance to lie close to the bottom. Straight and tight lines direct to the end tackle attract drifting weed and other muck like a magnet, and end up looking as if hung with washing.

Fixed and Running Leads

Before any specific rigs are discussed and recommended, let's first separate the theories and myths from the reality. First, when we refer to a 'running lead', what we really mean is that when the tackle has been cast in, the lead stays stationary and the line runs through it. The truth, however, is that running rigs very rarely run when they're in the water, because unless we're using an extremely heavy weight of perhaps a half pound or more, or the lead is trapped on the bottom, when a fish pulls at the bait the lead will move: it will roll down the river, or be carried down the river by the fish – *the line will not be running through the lead.* Even if we were to achieve a perfectly straight line from rod tip to the bait, with no angle where the line runs through the lead, it is still very unlikely the line will run, because the fish also has to pull at the bait in the same straight line. Even the most subtle angle is enough to make the lead move, rather than the line drawing through it.

The Running Rig

So why bother with a running rig if it offers no advantages over a fixed or semi-fixed rig? Because it presents advantages other than the theoretical one of offering little or no resistance to a bite. The main advantage is one of conservation, in that if the main line should break through abrasion or for some other reason, the lead will slide free and the barbel will not become tethered. There are also occasions when a barbel has to be played through a weedbed, and often the lead or feeder slides along the line rather than being pulled into the weed, and thus there is less chance of the tackle becoming snagged.

A further point where running rigs are concerned is that a running rig can easily be made into a semi-fixed rig simply with the addition of a silicon float stop on the line somewhere above the lead. So if you're not completely sold on the idea that running rigs don't run, you can use the silicon stop to prevent the line from running through the lead or feeder, yet be safe in the knowledge that the stop will slide off should the lead become snagged. The silicon stop should be applied either tight to the lead or feeder, trapping it against the swivel stop to present a rig where the line is not able to run, or a few

inches away for a rig where the line can run a little on the bite and then become fixed shortly after to present the bolt effect.

The Fixed Rig

The idea of using a fixed rig is to present a bolt effect: when a barbel takes the bait it is met with firm resistance, the hook pricks it, and the fish bolts, completing the process of hooking the fish – hence the reason why bolt rigs are often called self-hooking rigs. The reality, however, is as has been described above, in that the lead moves regardless of whether it's fixed or not when downstream legering, which is the most common direction to leger, and a barbel will come up against the resistance from the rod tip anyhow. Yet whether you accept that fact or not, there are still circumstances that present good reasons for using a fixed rig.

Most fixed rigs use a safety clip to attach the lead or feeder to the line. The safety clip retains leads and feeders up to about 5oz when casting, but will discharge them should they become snagged. So regardless of the bolt rig theory, there is a case for using a lead clip if you're fishing a weedy swim where there is more than a slim chance of becoming snagged. It may be better for the lead to be ejected and leave the

This simple running rig has a silicon float stop threaded on the line above lead; normally it would be moved further away from the lead, but it is shown closer for clarity.

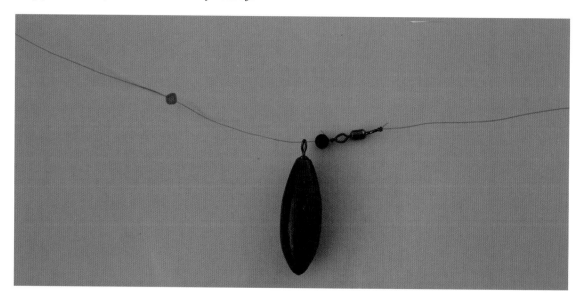

tackle free to play the fish, rather than have a running lead become snagged and be playing the fish via the line running through the lead or feeder.

So you can see there is a case for both rigs, with the choice depending partly on your beliefs regarding leads and running lines in water, and partly on the proximity of snags and whether or not you're fishing close to them or right in them.

Swimfeeder Fishing

The use of swimfeeders was developed on the Thames as a method for catching dace in LAA Shield matches, but the anglers using them soon found that the constant stream of bait attracted chub and barbel, too, and it didn't take long for them to transfer the method to the popular barbel waters of the time such as the Hampshire Avon and the rapidly improving middle Severn. The swimfeeder method had the most impact on the Severn, where the vast shoals of barbel in the 2lb to 6lb bracket were voracious feeders.

Whichever type of feeder you choose, it is important to understand that feeder fishing won't work to its full potential unless you fish the swimfeeder as it is meant to be fished, and the clue is in its name: primarily a swimfeeder is

This is a fixed, but safe, non-tethering rig.

a means to feed the fish, and only a leger weight as a secondary consideration. To fish a feeder properly you have to understand the basic principles behind its use. Too many anglers fish a feeder by casting it every half hour or so, which is nonsense, because a feeder has to be cast at regular and frequent intervals to get the best out of it. The idea is to maintain a constant flow of

A specialized open-end feeder with an extra heavy loading to help hold bottom in powerful and flooded rivers such as the Trent, Wye, Ribble and Severn.

bait down the current in a quite narrow lane, a lane that will, following a period of filling and casting the feeder, create a quite lengthy feeding area, one that extends for possibly twenty yards or more downstream from the casting point. Any fish that happens upon the feeding lane, at any point along it, will be tempted to follow the lane to its source, which is the feeder itself and, lying just below it, your hookbait.

If, for reasons to do with disturbing the swim, you think regular casting is not part of your plan, then you would do better introducing loose feed by some other method – by hand or catapult, bait dropper or PVA bag, for instance.

Today we have three types of swimfeeder: the block-end, the open end (or groundbait feeder as they're often known), and the Method feeder (*see* Chapter 9).

Block-End Feeder Fishing

The type of feeder that has proved the most successful for barbel fishing, particularly for shoal barbel in the 2lb to 6lb bracket, is the block-end feeder. It is ideal for the particle approach, which for many years meant using maggots or casters, usually mixed with hempseed. In more recent years it has become common to mix in small pellets as well, usually in the 2–3mm size.

Block-end feeders are available in a variety of sizes, from ones taking just a dozen or so

'Dead cow' add-on feeder leads are available in various shapes and sizes. Make sure the ones you buy fit the feeders that you intend to attach them to.

maggots to jumbo-sized ones that take a large handful. There are two basic shapes, cylindrical and oval, with the oval shape holding bottom a little better than the round ones, which are more inclined to roll. The popularity of the block-end method on the middle Severn, especially around Bewdley, led local tackle dealer Mal Storey to develop specialist feeders that were big and robust enough for the rigours of the streamy Severn. Furthermore, many anglers sought a means to add extra weight to the standard feeder loadings so that a variety of special add-on weights for feeders were designed to replace the home-made efforts using roofing lead. The proprietary trim weights are known as 'cow leads'. These add-on leads are essential aids to river swimfeeder fishing.

The size and weight of the feeder is not the only consideration, especially when using inanimate baits such as caster, hemp and pellet. Unlike maggots, which can easily crawl out of the holes in the feeder, we have to rely on the current and the size of the holes to make sure inanimate baits can escape. Anglers use knives, scissors and drill bits to increase the size of the existing holes, but a much better method is to use the device made for the job, the 'John Roberts feeder hole enlarger'.

The frequency of casting, the size of the feeder, and the rate at which the feeder empties, all combine to regulate how much bait, and at what rate, it is fed into the swim. This important factor needs to be given considerable thought, because it is the main element in a technique that depends on correct feeding to work properly. The first consideration is the weight of the feeder, because it must be heavy enough to hold bottom *after the feeder has emptied*; it must also be large enough to feed the quantity of bait you think is right, and with holes of the right number and the right size to allow the bait to escape at the correct rate – not too fast and not too slowly: too fast, and the feed will go down the swim as a mass, too slowly and it will trickle down too sparsely. In an unknown swim you should make a few experimental casts until you get the weight and the feeding rate exactly as you want it.

From that point on you are dictated to by how well the barbel are feeding, and should

This useful selection of block-end feeders covers the best sizes for barbel fishing. Some of them can be modified by enlarging the holes using a John Roberts hole enlarger.

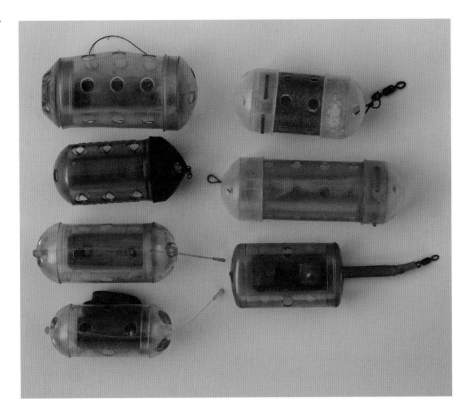

regulate the feed accordingly. What you don't do is cast less often with the same amount of feed. The best way to reduce the feed is to reduce the amount you put into the feeder, *but always cast at the same rate.* Good swimfeeder fishing is all about casting timing and rhythm: get it right, and the fish can be coerced into a feeding pattern that has been triggered by food that appears in a familiar and habit-forming sequence.

Open-End Feeders

All the above recommendations for block-end swimfeeder fishing apply to open-end feeders, except there is no need to modify the holes as the current flowing through the open ends dictates the rate at which the feed is dispensed – that, and the fact that open-end feeders are used more for feeding groundbait, with a liberal lacing of hookbaits such as sweetcorn, small cubes of meat, other larger-than-particle baits and, in particular for barbel fishing, damp pellets. An extra factor in the feed rate consideration is the consistency of the groundbait or

damp pellet mix. These can be made so that they disperse at different rates according to their dryness or solidity. The addition of ground hempseed will assist groundbait and damp pellets to burst out of the feeder.

Feeder Rigs

You don't need anything special for feeder rigs: the running rig and fixed rig described above are just as good for feeder fishing as they are for lead fishing.

Roving for Barbel

Walking the river is an enjoyable thing to do even when you haven't got any tackle and bait with you, and it's surprising what you learn about fish just by walking and observing. Set out on a nice evening, when the water is clear, the weed is lush, and bank-side trees and vegetation are in full bloom: these are the best conditions for fish spotting and laying traps for later in the evening when all goes quiet except for the hooting of owls and the occasional splash of those big barbel that now feel safe, and hungry, under the cover of darkness.

Of course, that is the idyllic setting, and the one we would wish upon ourselves if only we could. Idyllic or not, though, roving the river for barbel can be a deadly approach if you go about it the right way.

The first thing to get right is to choose a stretch of river that lends itself to roving. There is no point in roving a very popular stretch where most swims are likely to be taken, or where there is a good chance that any swim you've pre-baited will be occupied when you arrive to fish it. The roving approach involves pre-baiting swims, and is a method best

These large open-end feeders have a heavy lead loading and the capacity to deposit plenty of feed on the river bed.

Take advantage of cover when roving.

followed on quiet stretches where the barbel are big but few in number, and where location is the most difficult element. There are two ways you can go about it: one is to rove through the day and fish for each barbel you spot or each likely swim you come across. The alternative is to walk the river and pick from three to half-a-dozen likely swims, and pre-bait these in readiness to fish later in the day, or (more likely) for a dusk and through-the-night session.

Travel Light

Whichever roving approach you decide on, you need to travel as light as possible to gain maximum enjoyment. Also, if you carry too much gear and bait you will be less inclined to move on when you really know the time is right. Two rods is one too many, but you will need a landing net and a small rucksack holding all your end tackle and other bits and pieces. If it's a short session you can do without the flask and sandwiches, the chair and any other comforts – use your unhooking mat to sit on. For a longer, all night session, a lightweight chair and some refreshments are essential. Other than that you need an adequate supply of bait (especially if you've chosen the pre-baiting approach), which you can carry in a canvas bait bucket.

Bait and Feed

For the roving approach, and because of having to travel as light as possible, it is wise to choose just a small selection of hookbaits and one type of feedbait – you need an adequate supply of bait, which means you can't afford to be taking sufficient quantities of different baits. Most barbel will respond to hemp and micro pellet as feed, and if you take a small selection of hookbaits such as sweetcorn, luncheon meat, pellets and boilies, and maybe a few lobworms if the water has recently flooded, you are well covered. However, more than likely you will be fishing a stretch you know well, so you can probably narrow down the bait choice even more to one or two baits that you know are certainties for that stretch.

Feed the swims with any of the usual methods, by hand, catapult or bait dropper; a bait dropper is best for accuracy if the swim is within a rod's length or so from the bank because it is easy, even in darkness, to introduce more bait to exactly the same spot. Depending on the size of the dropper, put the equivalent of three or four good handfuls of mixed micro pellet and hempseed into each swim, along with a sprinkling of sweetcorn, larger pellets, boilies or whatever is your chosen hookbait. Alternatively, don't include any hookbait samples whatsoever, as there may be occasions when the best time to introduce a hookbait is when it's on the hook, offering the fish this different alternative to the free feed only when you are actually fishing.

It can pay to rove with a bait bucket and feed some swims prior to fishing them later in the day.

This is a particularly useful ploy when using large hookbaits such as boilies and luncheon meat. The value of such options can, of course, only be determined by trial and error over a period of time, but being aware of them is essential.

Swim by Swim
Rove the full length of the stretch of river you've chosen, and pre-bait up to half-a-dozen likely barbel swims along the way, although three or four swims are usually enough. When you reach the last swim and have introduced the bait, you wander back to the first swim you chose and begin fishing. By then there should have been a sufficient lapse in time for the barbel to have settled in, begun feeding, and gained enough confidence to believe they are 'safe'. If you have enough patience you can sit and wait for a while longer before casting a line to make sure the barbel are feeding undisturbed and confidently. If the swim is suitable for hand feeding, you can trickle a little bait in while you wait, providing you remain out of sight and the swim remains completely undisturbed apart from that discreet sprinkle of loose feed.

If the pre-baiting has done its job you usually don't have to wait long before you see some action. The usual feeding pattern for barbel is for them to visit a baited patch, the first time with all senses on red alert. They remain for a short spell, perhaps tentatively sampling one or two food items and then retreating for up to twenty minutes or so. If nothing has disturbed them, they'll return and stay a while longer, until eventually, now confidently feeding on the bait you've introduced, they will remain and settle in the swim for as long as it takes either to clear up the feed or to satisfy their hunger, whichever comes first. The longer you can leave it, within reason, between putting those bait droppers of hemp and pellet into the swim and introducing a hookbait, the better – providing you don't leave it so long they have time to mop it all up and abandon the swim for pastures new.

The timing of this procedure will vary from river to river, from swim to swim and from day to day. Only experience can teach you the right timing, but a good rule of thumb is to wait from about a half hour to one hour between baiting

and fishing. And based on what you learn over a season or two, you can adjust the amount of bait you put in and the length of time you wait.

How Long?
So how long do you fish one of those pre-baited swims before moving on to try the next one? Again this will vary, but if you've left the swim for at least a half hour since it was baited, you can expect a bite within about fifteen minutes of introducing a hookbait. This is often a lot less, and when everything has gone according to plan it isn't unusual to get that rod-wrenching bite almost immediately the bait settles on the bottom – providing you haven't unsettled the fish when you introduced it.

When you catch a fish, bait the swim with a few more droppers of feed and move to the next swim, working your way along the swims you've baited until eventually you can start again at swim number one. Of course, this all depends on how long you spend in each swim, how far apart they are, and how much time and energy you've got to devote to the task.

One Swim, One Bait
Finally, try at least one swim that hasn't been baited in any shape or form. Just drop your hookbait in, preferably a really big, strong-smelling, meaty bait that the barbel can detect easily. Many times the biggest barbel of a session has been caught in this way.

Night Fishing

Night fishing for barbel doesn't necessarily mean fishing all night. Plenty of barbel anglers fish from an hour or so before dusk and a few hours into darkness. On most rivers this is the best time to fish, and during high summer can mean just a few hours fishing if you intend going to work the next day. From late autumn, however, it means that you can start fishing at 4pm and stop fishing at, say, 10pm, and still be home in time for supper. If you are fishing part of the night or all night through, you must be well prepared for fishing the dark hours, especially in winter when the temperature drops rapidly at dusk.

A head torch is more than useful for night fishing.

Comfort is Key

Even in the height of summer you should take an extra jumper or jacket with you, because even the warmest summer days have a habit of dipping into much colder temperatures after dark, and you feel the cold all the more in darkness, especially when sat for long periods of doing very little but watching the rod. The real key to successfully fishing into darkness in winter is comfort. Whatever species you target, you will not fish for them consistently successfully unless you're comfortable and warm. Sat there restlessly shivering and wet is not the way to fish at your best.

Kit yourself out with thermal underwear, one or two layers of fleece, and top it off with either a one-piece suit, or a jacket and trouser or bib and brace, waterproof, breathable outer shell. Cover your head with a cap, and have a balaclava standing by for when conditions are really severe. Full, waterproof gloves are good for when you're carrying your gear, and a thinner glove, possibly fingerless, for when you're actually fishing. Finally, look after your feet with a pair of thermal socks, and a pair of very good quality waterproof walking boots. Plenty of warm layers, which can be peeled off or added as necessary, are a

blessing when roving, as you build up heat when on the move and soon lose it when you sit for a spell.

And what about a shelter? There are plenty of anglers who dress more or less as described above and happily fish with no cover at all from any kind of shelter. Of course, with good quality gear they stay perfectly dry and warm throughout all kinds of weather. Some, however, do at least sit under an umbrella. No matter how much the right clothing keeps you dry and warm some of us still much prefer to look at poor weather from under cover, being quite willing to sacrifice a little fishing efficiency for the sake of that greater feeling of well-being. But that's up to the individual, and not everyone feels the same way.

This winter night fishing, even if it's only a few hours into darkness, can be very enjoyable if you go about it the right way. With modern clothing and equipment you can be just as warm and comfortable as you are on many a summer's evening. So why miss the chance of some great fishing simply because it's cold and dark when it's so easy to make those two elements practically count for nothing?

Mark landed this double-figure Stour fish just after dusk, a classic summer barbel feeding time.

At night it is best to fish swims you've come to know well through fishing them in daylight, because then you know exactly where to cast so that your bait is lying in that certain area you've learned is the hotspot. A lot of night fishing is done through feel and instinct, but you can only get that feel and instinct for a swim by fishing it frequently in daylight and thereby acquiring the necessary knowledge. Night fishing enhances that feel, because when your vision is impaired your other instincts come to the fore.

Always arrive at your swim with at least an hour of daylight to spare; that way you can check if any snags have been washed into any of the swims you intend to fish, and equally important, can give yourself time to bait up accurately and settle in before darkness. Night fishing can be a dangerous game at any time for the in-experienced, but even the experienced night fisher has to take sensible precautions.

Barbel often haunt the same swims in dark-ness as in daylight, but many times they feed in the shallower water at night, often close to the margins, darkness providing the essential feeling of security, false though it may be as far as anglers are concerned. So if you have spotted

barbel in shallow water but have only succeeded in scaring them away when you've tried to catch them, try these same swims at night, because the cover of darkness may be all the fish need to give them the confidence to feed in shallow water.

Tackle

The rod, reel, line and end tackle you use at night need not be any different to what you use in daylight. Barbel don't fight any differently in darkness, although it often seems that way when you're visually impaired and your senses are on touch alert. One essential addition to the rod is a betalight, which is fixed to the rod tip with a special silicon adaptor.

This type of indicator is very good in short doses, because after a while betalights begin to play tricks on your eyes, and you imagine you're seeing bites when in reality the tip has hardly moved. They are especially prone to this when there is a wind and the tip is moving from the wind action. The answer is to not look directly at the betalight, but to see it through your peripheral vision. Look anywhere, providing you see the betalight from only the corner of your eye. You'll know when you have a bite just as surely as if you were looking directly at it. Using two betalight attachments, spaced about 4in to 6in apart, is better. Shining a discreet torch beam on to the rod tip is better still, but the problem is that your night vision is never allowed to develop, and once you look away from the rod tip you are almost totally blind for some time after, which is a disadvantage when you come to play and net a fish. Most night anglers use a head torch for baiting up and tackle changes.

Even more important when night fishing, and always handy even in daylight, is to have at least half-a-dozen hook lengths already tied and stored in a rig wallet. Although it is easy enough to tie rigs in darkness under the light of a head torch, it's something you can well do without. And it's a good idea to use rigs that incorporate a quick-change link so the hook-length changes are swift and simple. Another plus factor of such a set-up is that you can have a hook length already baited, making re-baiting swift and simple too.

Make sure you put your landing net in a handy spot and preferably away from where rats can get at the mesh: they love to chew their way through mesh that stinks of fish, particularly when you've just caught a fish and there is fresh slime on it. The same applies to bait and your tackle box: keep it by you and easily accessible. Place your chair so that your rod lies close to your hand, presuming that you won't always be holding it. The aim is to make any procedure in darkness easy and second nature.

Baits

As far as baits are concerned you don't need anything special. All the same considerations apply as in daylight, except that very visual baits such as bright yellow sweetcorn, which some big barbel may shy away from in daylight, could be well worth a try in darkness. The same applies to luncheon meat, in that some big, nervous barbel actually flee from it in daylight but may be tempted to take it under the cover of darkness.

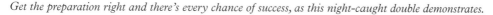

Get the preparation right and there's every chance of success, as this night-caught double demonstrates.

9 OTHER RIGS AND METHODS

Upstream Legering

The most common legering style is to cast across and downstream of the angler's position, with enough weight to hold bottom and with a slight bend in the rod tip due to the current pushing on the line. This is the case no matter how high the rod is positioned, for there is always some line in the water. Bites are indicated by the rod tip being suddenly bent into a larger curve or, less often, when the rod tip springs back as the line is relieved of weight.

Another method, and a highly sensitive one at that, is to fish upstream of the angler's position, but not too far across. To fish this method correctly, the balance of the end tackle has to be precise. The aim is for the leger weight to only just hold bottom, with only a slight change needed in the forces being applied to the weight to make it shift position. The method can be used with a swimfeeder, but is best fished with a bait that will discharge from it quickly and the feeder finely tuned (a strip of roofing lead is a good material for this) to hold bottom after emptying. The ultimate aim is to present a bait that if disturbed only a little by a fish, will cause the tackle to dislodge, move downstream and hook the fish, or at least prick the fish causing it to bolt and hook itself. Bites are usually indicated by the rod tip registering a slight pull and then springing back as the tension is removed from it.

The procedure is to cast to the desired position with a weight that you estimate is right, and then adjust the weight up or down in successive casts until it is holding bottom. Then tighten the line slowly (unless the force of the current is sufficient) until there is a slight bend in the rod top. A number of anglers use a quivertip for upstream legering as it is easier to set a more significant bend in it than it is in a rod tip – perhaps one of the few occasions when a quivertip is an advantage when barbel fishing. You'll need to increase the amount of weight again if,

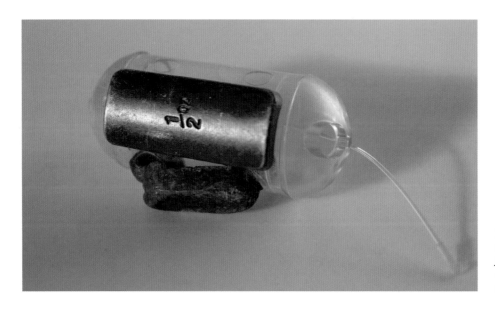

This medium size block-end feeder has additional lead added.

Barbel bites are usually rod benders, but this quiver tip will register even the more hesitant ones.

after setting the bend in the tip, it dislodges too easily. You can make fine adjustments to the tension in the line by altering the amount of line that is in the water through raising or lowering the rod. Remember, the idea is to balance the amount of weight against the current so that it takes only the slightest pull on the weight to shift it.

When a fish does take the bait, no matter how subtly, the weight will dislodge and immediately drift downstream, and the fish will go with it as this is its natural movement; at this stage the fish may not even know it has a baited hook in its mouth. Following the bite, the tip will spring back and the line will fall slack, and you will often find that you have to retrieve line at quite a fast rate to get back in touch with the fish. Once you do feel the fish, that is the time to strike, to make sure the hook has a good hold.

It makes no difference, as far as execution of the method is concerned, if the rig is running or fixed, because the lead is going to move anyway;

after all, that's the whole concept of the method! A longer-than-usual hook length seems to work better when upstreaming, maybe due to the bait being further away from the main line to the leger weight, for both will be coming away from the same point, although the main line will be angled towards the bank and the hook length directly downstream.

Try upstream legering when you can't cast to the swim from an upstream position, or when you want maximum sensitivity. Be patient when setting up, as the method is far more critical of balance from rod tip to leger weight than any other legering method.

The Rolling Leger

The rolling leger method, or 'trundling' as it is sometimes known, is exactly that: a leger weight that is allowed, indeed encouraged, to roll along the river bed. It is used when it is not feasible to

Adjust the size of the weight to suit conditions when using the rolling leger.

float fish and a moving bait is wanted. A moving bait will often be taken by wary fish that haven't been given time to study and taste a bait that is being legered in a fixed position – it being a case of grab it or lose it! The rolling leger has become a much more popular method in recent years, and has accounted for a good number of barbel. It is more of a summer method than a winter one, because the barbel need to be on the move and searching for food for it to have maximum impact, and that is more likely to be in the higher water temperatures of the summer months and into autumn to some extent. Don't discount it for winter fishing, however, just be sure to choose the milder days to try it.

It helps greatly to have a good working knowledge of the stretch where you're going to fish the rolling leger method; and if you don't know it well, then it helps if the river waters are clear. There is no point in trying to roll a bait through a thick weedbed, or through an area that is riddled with snags, so at least choose a stretch where you can see the bottom if it's not a stretch you are familiar with.

Rolling Tackle

Like upstream legering, the tackle for rolling legering needs to be balanced to work properly, though not necessarily quite so finely balanced as the idea is to move from swim to swim where there will be some difference in bottom make-up, depth and flow rates. A running rig makes most sense, as this is a safe rig if the tackle becomes snagged, which is always more likely when it is constantly on the move. Many barbel anglers advocate using a drilled bullet or some other round lead with a hole through its centre, claiming that such leads enable the tackle to roll more smoothly. But that is truer in theory than it is in reality, as any lead will 'roll' down the swim if it isn't heavy enough to remain in position. Of course, flat leads will hold better than round leads, but only just, and the difference is so negligible it's neither here nor there.

A good compromise is to use a round bomb with a built-in swivel. To describe the method as 'rolling' is somewhat deceiving anyway, because the lead rarely rolls, as such, but rather bounces down the current in a variety of bumps and slides. It's important to use a quick-change clip to attach the leger weight so that weights can be changed as easily and fast as possible in order to fish either heavier or lighter. In many swims it is possible either to freeline, or to use a varying number of SSG shot on a link. There is usually no need to fish on the light side where lines are concerned, as the bait will be on the move, giving the barbel less chance to inspect the end tackle and become suspicious.

Rolling Baits

The rolling leger method is often known as the 'rolling meat' method, as meat is the bait most often used – although there is no reason whatsoever why it can't be fished with any bait normally used for barbel. Natural baits such as lobworms, prawns, minnows and slugs are excellent for summer and autumn, with luncheon meat, other meats, boilies and pellets coming into their own from autumn onwards. Maggot and caster are worth a try at any time of the year.

Rolling Leger Technique

With this method it is essential to regulate the speed of the bait's movement through the water, as a bait that doesn't make a natural progression either along the bottom, or higher in the water if that's where you think the barbel are feeding, will only serve to alert their suspicions. In clear water you can often see the barbel apparently chasing a bait down the current, but this behaviour is more akin to the barbel following the bait, rather than chasing it, as they watch its behaviour before deciding whether to take it or not.

In some slow swims you can actually freeline the bait, and this is the best way of all if the flow is light enough to enable you to do so, but on most rivers and in most swims you need some lead to slow down the bait enough so that it doesn't run through too fast. To give you an idea of how your bait should be travelling through the swim, throw in a few hookbait samples and watch their progress. In a current with some pace, smaller baits such as maggot, caster and sweetcorn will take a little time to reach bottom, and there are times when the barbel are well on feed that they will intercept the feed as it is still sinking.

The tackle needs to be balanced so that the lead just about holds bottom, but with only a little gentle persuasion will shift and glide downstream. Cast slightly upstream, wait for the lead to settle and hold, and then allow two or three yards of line to peel from the reel. Then with little flicks of the rod tip you can start the tackle rolling again, holding the rod with one hand and a loop of line between butt ring and reel draped over the fingers of your other hand.

ABOVE: Luncheon meat cut into sticks makes it easier to break off a chunk.

BELOW: John Searl concentrates hard as he watches barbel approach his bait in very clear water.

Moulding some 'Heavy Metal' tungsten putty to the hook shank will keep the bait on the bottom when using the rolling meat method.

As the tackle progresses downstream, in fits and starts and sometimes with prolonged rolls, keep in touch with it by pulling and extending the loop of line or relaxing it and allowing it to feed back through the rod. You can also manipulate the roll by either raising or lowering the rod so that the amount of line in the current varies. Another way is to build weight into the hook with Heavy Metal: bury the hook in a big chunk of meat, and freeline this down the swim, changing the way it behaves by varying the size of the meat and the amount of Heavy Metal applied to the hook.

There are times, in suitable swims, when you can give the bait its head by opening the bale arm and allowing the bait to roll for a fair distance, much the same as if you were trotting a bait down the swim.

With experience you will feel more in touch with the end tackle, and will know instinctively when to feed line and when to tighten it, when to allow the bait to settle for a few seconds, and when to start it rolling again. It can be a fascinating way to fish, with almost as much tackle manipulation required as when float fishing. But it's a technique that requires practice, because like most skills, you only begin to enjoy it properly when you fully understand it and can fish it with skill and confidence.

Fishing the Method

'The Method' is a self-hooking fixed rig utilizing a short hook link to a special in-line feeder that has its outer surface loaded with groundbait. Although it is technically a fixed rig, it can, and should, be tied up so that the feeder will come free should the main line break. Don't use the elasticated feeders favoured by match anglers, as these are not suitable for barbel and could leave a fish tethered. Bury the hookbait in the groundbait on the feeder, the idea being that the fish attacks the ball of feed and subsequently unearths the hookbait and takes it into its mouth along with the free feed.

Ideally the Method feeder should be used with much the same procedure as any swim-feeder, in that it should be cast regularly and used to build up feed in a swim in order to encourage the fish to feed with confidence. By its very nature it is a heavy, aggressive and noisy means of fishing, but it can pay dividends in the right swim at the right time. It is not a method that can be fished in the way it was meant to be fished when targeting big, very wary barbel, and especially not in clear chalk streams. It is a method that is most suited to fishing for small to medium-sized barbel found in shoals of more than half a dozen or so, and preferably even larger, and in bigger rivers.

Most barbel anglers tend to use the Method by leaving it out for long periods of more than

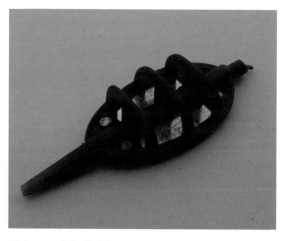

This type of flat bed Method feeder is ideal for Method feeder fishing for barbel.

an hour or so, because of the disturbance of regular casting, but this rather defeats the object, because after several minutes the groundbait will have dissolved off the feeder and been washed downstream, leaving just a big feeder and the hookbait. If the groundbait or dampened pellets have been mixed so that they won't dissolve after several minutes, then again it is defeating the object, because not enough feed will be trickling off it to attract the fish from downstream.

The Method is meant to be an 'instant' fish catcher, and if you haven't caught a fish on it after a few minutes then it's time to draw in, load the feeder, and cast in again. The Method does catch barbel, but unless it is used as it is meant to be used, it is probably catching fish in spite of it being 'the Method' rather than because of it, and is merely just another device that does no more than feed the swim.

It can be used with any of the usual barbel baits and any of the usual Method mix groundbaits or dampened pellets; the hook link can also be made from any of the materials used in other rigs, but should be kept short, preferably around 4in.

Fishing Weirs

'Don't Judge a Book by Its Cover'
Although many small weirs – or mill pools, if you prefer – are lovely, peaceful places to fish, some larger weirs give the impression that they are really fearsome, with rushing, gushing water powering over the sill, cascading on to the apron and then exploding into white foam. From there the current charges down the centre before dividing into two distinct flows that usually turn and then flow back gently towards the apron.

This small River Dane weirpool has plenty of snags, making it ideal territory for barbel.

This Hampshire Avon weirpool is vast compared to the River Dane one, yet still small compared to some big river weirs.

Many anglers are put off fishing weirs because they seem so formidable, yet the old adage of 'not judging a book by its cover' is very true, because what goes on beneath the surface can be entirely different to what you see in front of you. The only true way to read a weir is to fish it and see what happens to your tackle. Watch how your float sometimes follows the surface water, and at other times travels in the opposite direction. Note how your leger weight will stay put in some really powerful-looking swims, and yet will roll out of others that look exactly the same. A weir can change regularly as floodwater carries in more debris and cuts different paths in the bottom, so never be surprised if your float or leger doesn't behave in the same way every time you fish there.

A Variety of Swims
Weirs offer a great variety of swims. Even where the white water crashes on to the apron can be an excellent place to fish, because the apron is there to protect the bottom from being gouged out from that mad rush of water, and below it is

an undercut where the water is fairly calm, no more than a gentle turbulence. Barbel, fish that are built to withstand strong currents, love to lie below the apron, sliding out to feed in the turbulence for a minute or two, before gliding back under for a spell of respite. The central flow is strongest, but even there the bottom is nothing like as powerful as the surface, and again, barbel forage there. The side eddies can hold barbel too at times, when they favour the gentle, almost still flow of water. The creases between the main flow and the side eddies are also always worth investigating, as is the run-off, or tail end, because barbel will feed there at some time or other.

Tackle for Snag Fishing
Weirs are notorious for being snaggy, because the intricacies of the currents ensure that all manner of flotsam and jetsam is carried round in the eddies and backflows until it becomes waterlogged and sinks. Although these snags are a disadvantage in so far as they can be tackle-devouring monsters, they can also be an

advantage, for they are usually hotspots, especially for barbel. Location of barbel certainly becomes easier, in that it is a case of find the snags and you find the barbel.

It pays to fish weirs with at least slightly heavier tackle than you would normally use in that same river. For instance, where 10lb line would be your norm for barbel fishing, then use 11lb test, or even 12lb in the weir, especially if you intend fishing a snag swim. There are snags in a River Dane weir that many anglers tackle with 15lb line. Always be sure that your tackle is safe, too, with in-built 'rotten bottoms' when using a link to the leger weight or feeder, and set up in such a way that barbel cannot become tethered. Make sure you use a rod that can handle the heavier line.

Feeding in a Weir

Feeding the swim in a weir is probably the most difficult aspect to get right. Loose feeding is a real gamble, because the surface flow can carry the bait away from where you want it to end up,

which means that loose feeding has the reverse effect, acting as a magnet that draws fish away from the swim rather than towards it. This leaves us with three options: first, when legering with small particle baits such as maggot, caster and hemp, use a swimfeeder, and preferably one with extra weight (over and above what is needed to hold bottom), because it will cut through the fast surface water, sink fast, and get the bait distributed along the bottom. The extra weight will also go some way to making sure the feeder stays put once it hits bottom, as you don't want the tackle rolling round the swim if it's the usual snaggy weir environment. If necessary, tape over some of the holes in the feeder to prevent too much of the feed escaping as it sinks. It is better to begin with too little feed escaping (which you can establish by casting and retrieving at different time spans) and gradually expose more holes, than to spread too much feed around in the surface area, which could risk it ending up where you don't want it.

The famous Great Weir on the Royalty Fishery holds barbel even if the backdrop is far from scenic.

Big, solid baits such as cubes of luncheon meat, boilies, larger pellets, sections of sausage and pepperami, can be fed with a stringer or PVA bag. Even the fastest dissolving PVA isn't fast enough to melt before the bait hits bottom. PVA bags and stringers can be used in slow-flowing swims, too, because other than a swim-feeder there are few better ways of ensuring the loose feed lies close to the hookbait – unless you are fishing within a rod's length or so, when a bait dropper will do a good job.

Locating Barbel in Weirs

The white water below the apron is a favourite barbel haunt, but there will be one or more hotspots along that apron where you will catch more barbel than anywhere else. There may be a boulder that provides a food trap, or a slightly deeper hole that also holds more food than other areas. Most often the only way of finding these features is to fish each spot along the apron over a period of several weeks, or longer, and see what transpires.

The main rush of water down the centre of the weir is the next place to try – in fact in certain conditions it should be the first place to cast a bait. This centre flow is usually the deepest spot, and later in the day, in summer when the sun is high, it can be where the barbel move to following an early morning feed under the apron. The side eddies are best when the water is high and coloured following a spell of heavy rain. And side eddies can be very productive in the evenings, regardless of conditions. Finally, if there are snags in any of the swims then it is almost certain you will find barbel in and around them.

It will probably take a couple of seasons before you have a detailed picture of a weir, before you are able to predict with any certainty where you will take barbel in a variety of conditions.

Fish the rod set high when legering weirs. It is important to keep as much line as possible out of the water between rod tip and end tackle so that those strong surface currents are kept away

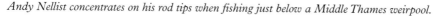

Andy Nellist concentrates on his rod tips when fishing just below a Middle Thames weirpool.

Dusk on the Trent – carbelling in style. (Courtesy of Bob Roberts)

from the line. Even with minimum line in the water there will be many times when you least expect it that the line will fall slack. It could be a bite, but is more likely to be the myriad of currents in a weir at work, at one time pushing firmly at the line and at other times hardly making any difference. When the line falls slack, take it up a little on the reel so that you're always in touch.

Carbelling

Carbelling is a term that's been coined to describe fishing for barbel with carp fishing gear and tactics; however, all barbel fishing is based a little on carp fishing. True carbelling is when it is taken a stage further, with two heavier-than-normal rods, kitted out with heavier-than-normal reels and lines, and fished with bite alarms, possibly on a rod pod. Carbelling is used mainly on the lower reaches of the big rivers such as the Severn and especially the Trent along the tidal reaches. Some anglers use it on the smaller rivers, too, and the upper and middle reaches of the bigger rivers, but it looks

out of place and is usually unnecessary anyway. Very often it really *is* carp anglers with carp tackle who fancy a change of species, or are taking a sabbatical from carp fishing during the colder months.

Spotting barbel and casting to them on these deep lower reaches is about as feasible as carbelling on a chalk stream, so it's a case of horses for courses, although the purist barbel angler is unlikely to see it like that. Nevertheless, on the lower reaches of the big rivers it makes a lot of sense to fish carbelling style, because there are usually few features to discern one swim from another (although there are still hotspots), and the best way to catch barbel is to lay a well baited trap and fish two baits in it with rods and lines that can deal with the weight and the wear and tear.

Tackle for Carbelling
Heavy barbel rods or light carp rods? The 'label' provided by the manufacturer will tell you which is which, but the truth is that they will probably be one and the same. Rods of a minimum of 1¾lb test curve, and better still in some swims, 2lb TC, and 12ft long, are about right.

Use free-spool reels in 5000 size loaded with 12–15lb line, and your favourite 'safe' rig with a heavy swimfeeder or gripper lead attached, terminating in a hook link of 12lb or so. Two pairs of long rod rests, a rod pod that can be elevated skywards, or the sea angler's tripod-type rod rest fitted with a pair of bite alarms, completes the set-up.

Baits

Although any of the usual barbel baits can be used, the larger, smellier varieties, such as pellets, boilies, meats and pastes, seem to be more successful. Pellets and boilies can be soaked or merely dipped in a strong flavour, and wraps of paste used over them to add to the attraction. Lobworms or a bunch of dendrobaena worms are always worth a try, especially during or following a spate.

Method

In big rivers you can afford to bait up quite heavily, because there is a much larger expanse from which to draw fish into your swim. In depths less than about 12ft (4m) you can take another leaf from the carp angler's book and use a spod to feed the swim, perhaps feeding a spod mix of various sized pellets, particles, and particularly hemp, to create a bed of feed. In deeper water it's probably better to use a swimfeeder, as the spread of bait from a spod could be too great when it has further to fall to reach bottom. The swimfeeder, even at low water, will most likely be a minimum of 2oz and should be filled, cast and retrieved continually for the first ten to fifteen minutes to create that bed of feed. Mesh-type open-end feeders are best, filled with soaked pellets along with hemp and other particles. The mix needs to be stiff enough to fall

An eleven-pounder from the Trent that fell to the 'carbelling' approach.

The river Severn is ideal for the carbelling approach.

through the water without dispensing, but not too stiff as it will take too long to wash out once it hits bottom. Some trial and error will be necessary the first time you fish a swim.

Following the baiting period, you cast and feed as you would with any swimfeeder method, with a regularity and a rhythm, and only varying the amount you put in the feeder to suit the activity in the swim on the day. The other baiting alternative is with PVA stringers or bags, but a stringer restricts you to a certain type of feed, and PVA bags do not feed with the same gradual dispensing rate, and can't be used with wet feed such as hemp. Whether you use a feeder or a lead, it's best to fish at least a little overweight and keep the feed in as tight a bait lane as possible. There is a case for spreading the feed a little at the start of the session and then narrowing it down later: a few spods of bait to begin with, and then swapping to the feeder.

The lower reaches of big rivers are deep and generally have deceptively powerful currents, so rods need to be set high, with minimum line in the water. Although most of the time you will be watching your rod tips for bites, it's wise to set the free spools to release line, not just for safety reasons but to allow you to relax and watch the water and be able to tend to mixing bait, making rigs or hook links, and anything else you can feasibly do while waiting for some action. But don't forget to keep up that baiting rhythm if you're fishing a swimfeeder!

10 SEASONAL CHANGES AND EXTREME CONDITIONS

Seasonal Changes

Some anglers don't fish for barbel until the new season has been under way for several weeks; indeed, some don't bother until autumn, thinking that barbel are not at their best until then. Much of that opinion, however, is not based on how fit the barbel are, but more on whether they're going to be at their best (heaviest) weight. The heaviest weight a barbel can reach is not necessarily an indication of its condition, but more of the food availability in the river and how easily the barbel has been able to take advantage of that food. Autumn and winter floodwater conditions usually do most to boost barbel weights. As far as many anglers are concerned, the potential weight of the barbel is the one and only criterion, as they put the weight of fish at the top of their list of essentials.

It's a different matter if the barbel are not back to their best condition following spawning; however, their being rather thin is not a bad thing, but a quite natural result of that activity. As soon as they're fully fit, thin or not, they can offer some great sport – and need our baits most to help them put the pounds and ounces back on. If you just enjoy barbel fishing, and have no compulsion to seek barbel at their heaviest potential weight, then there is no reason whatsoever not to fish for them from the day the season opens in mid June. There are more reasons why this is good for the barbel's welfare than there are reasons against it.

Early Season
Barbel fishing in the early season is an experimental time, when the first task is to discover the location of the fish. Most often there will be

High summer: the weed is at full growth and the days are bright.

very little change from the time you stopped fishing in mid March, but in those three months new weed will have grown, some old weedbeds may no longer exist, and floodwater may have moved one or two snags and deposited others. Some undercut banks may be cut deeper and new ones formed, while others may have collapsed and no longer exist. Following spawning there could be some barbel that will seek out new territory. So the early season is a time to be on the move, taking advantage of the usual low and clear water to spot fish and features.

Most of us will be fishing stretches of river we know well and that often have banker swims where we know barbel reside almost permanently, but it is still a good idea to take a stroll before choosing a swim, to look out for any changes.

Through Summer

As the season progresses you can begin to take note of worn banks, indicating the swims used most often by anglers as chairs, boots and banksticks begin to wear away the vegetation and grass. There are two ways to consider these worn spots: one is to look on them as signs of good barbel swims, for surely they wouldn't be so worn if anglers continually blanked in them; and the other is to look on them as places to avoid, as they may have been used recently and the barbel in that area consequently well fed, especially if the late incumbent has tossed in all the bait he had left at the end of his session. If that's the case, then the barbel may not be up for feeding again for the next twenty-four hours or more. Sometimes there is even fresh bait spilt on the bank – but that would have to have been a swim in *very* recent use, as animals, rodents and birds usually don't take long to clear up these bounties. Popular swims can be good places to fish, in that the fish are always well fed and therefore conditioned to seeking food there; or they can be poor places to fish, because the bigger, warier barbel could be shy from the possible danger.

Of course, if your stretch of river is one of those that is little fished then you don't have such problems to take into consideration, but unfortunately not all stretches of river are like that and previous activity has to be taken into

This quiet and private stretch of the Hampshire Avon makes it easy to get far from the madding crowds.

account. You may be lucky in that you have a good choice of stretches on several rivers that vary between being very little fished to being very popular and quite busy on a daily basis. The popular stretches will be the easiest, as you would expect, so if you have little time to spare and just want to catch a few fish, then these are the obvious choice. At other times, when you have the time and you relish the challenge, you can visit the little fished stretches, hope you can find fish, and then present them with a bait that they'll accept.

Even if you're not into stalking and roving, but much prefer to settle in a swim and feed it to try and attract any barbel in the vicinity, taking a walk along the river before deciding on a swim is a wise move anyway. Half an hour spent strolling and fish spotting can be worth several hours

Early autumn; with weed dying back the water levels have dropped.

of fishing blind, possibly in a swim that is devoid of barbel. And you can always practise the old trick of pre-baiting a few likely swims as you come across them, and then fish each in turn as you see fit and according to what develops.

As the summer progresses, the barbel become more conditioned to feeding. The bait will have been going in regularly in most of the popular swims, and although the barbel may be more wary in some respects, they may yet be more inclined to feed. On a variety of rivers, the flow will have dropped noticeably by late summer. Weed growth stops, and as the weed starts to die it is less tough. On a number of shallow rivers the weed helps to hold up the water level, so as it dies back the level drops. On some shallow rivers, it means that some swims that had sufficient depth and flow to hold barbel at the start of the season, are now too shallow for the barbel to feel safe.

Late summer barbel fishing is often patchy; there are times when it is a struggle to find a barbel, never mind catch one, and others when the barbel seemingly go mad and everyone does well. At this time of year the conditions are likely to be very good at times, either for float fishing or a swimfeeder approach using hemp and caster.

Autumn

Autumn is a settling-down period on most rivers, and another reason why a number of barbel anglers don't bother to fish for the species until late September. Through September and October the barbel haunts and feeding patterns have become well established. Regular routines for both barbel and barbel anglers become settled, and the pattern is set until the first frosts begin to bite.

Winter

The change in seasons of course doesn't happen suddenly, with one shutting off one day and another beginning the next: each season blends

RIGHT: *In conditions as extreme as this, your best bet is to go for true cold-water fish such as chub or grayling – it depends how keen and optimistic you are!*

BELOW: *A digital thermometer that will tell you the actual temperature and the trend.*

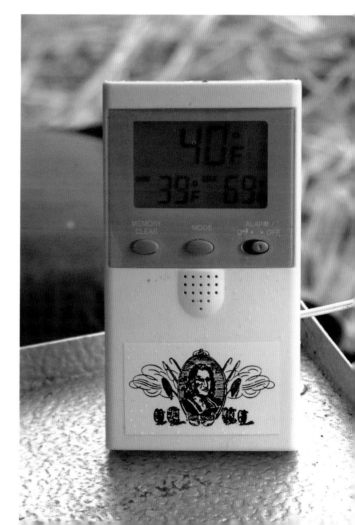

gradually into the other. In summer, you fish into the late evening in short sleeves, and then *seemingly* suddenly you find that you need long sleeves and then an extra pullover, and before you realize it, padded waterproof jackets and trousers are being worn as a matter of course – and it hits you that winter has arrived. And it arrives with a vengeance when you find you are tearing a damp landing net from the frozen grass and a white frost glistens on the rod.

Winter barbel fishing can be tough, and the barbel angler must be prepared to suffer many more blank outings than at any other time of year. The good days, when it is relatively mild and coloured floodwater fills the river, can be very good; the fish are at their biggest and they often feed at their best as they take advantage of favourable conditions.

The actual approach to catching winter barbel, as far as rigs and baits are concerned, is not so different to what you would use in summer, except that you have to modify a few things to suit the conditions you're fishing, particularly in the amount of feed you use when that temperature is not moving in a favourable direction. Generally speaking the barbel will be found in the same swims as they are throughout the warmer months, except that heavy winter floodwater will create new swims that the barbel are sure to exploit.

The significant element that determines much of what happens as far as barbel and their feeding habits are concerned is water temperature.

Water Temperature

It is all too easy to take too much notice of exact water temperatures. You know the kind of thing: roach feed best at X°F, and so on. But when it comes to barbel feeding in winter, 45°F seems to be very significant, the point at which the situation takes a turn for the better or worse. More than 45° and you've definitely got a chance of catching them, less than 45° and your chances diminish rapidly with every falling degree. It's the trend, however, that is very important; 44° and rising can be excellent, whereas 46° and falling can be dire, with the speed of the temperature change regulating the enthusiasm, or otherwise, of the barbel's appetite. Due to taking a lot of notice of water temperature when barbel fishing in winter some barbel anglers will often take a couple of readings though the week just to keep an eye on the trend and the rate of change. A digital thermometer is the ideal tool, but any thermometer will do the job.

Of course, you can ignore water temperature if you intend to fish only those perfect days when the river is running coloured and the temperature is unseasonably mild and it's obvious the barbel are going to be on the prod. Great if you always want the odds to be on your side – there is nothing at all wrong with that. However, a real challenge is to catch barbel all through the winter, even when there is ice and snow around. Many barbel anglers have fished all through many a winter and caught barbel regularly right through from November to the end of the season, even fishing when the water temperature was below 40°F and cat ice was tinkling in the margins.

It is through actually barbel fishing constantly, no matter what the weather is doing, which teaches us how very significant that 45°F really is. It leads to a lot of blanks, but there is no better way of learning about how to catch barbel in winter than fishing all through at least one winter when nothing, absolutely nothing, deters you from having a go. The one thing that helps to keep you going is that you very occasionally get that rare fish when you least expect it, when the conditions are at their

When it's cold enough to freeze in the margins the chances of barbel are slim, though not impossible.

It's easy to see the big chub in this very clear water, but the barbel is more difficult to spot.

very worst. Fish at least one winter all through for barbel and you'll be armed with the valuable knowledge of at least one of your local rivers through winter. In subsequent winters, watch the weather, and the trend of the weather, keep an eye on the water temperature, and go barbel fishing when you know you have at least a reasonable chance of catching them.

Extreme Conditions

Throughout the seasonal changes outlined above the atmospheric and water conditions will vary, but there are two extremes that have to be dealt with, which require a different approach to the usual one. Extreme river conditions are when the river runs low and clear, especially in the southern chalk streams, when practically every pebble on the bottom can be counted. The other extreme is the thick and fierce flood-water that follows heavy rain, especially in spate rivers, that turns to the colour of stewed tea and brings down tree branches, dead sheep and other debris in its wake. Both extremes have their negative aspects, clear water making every-thing highly visible and placing the barbel on high alert as they use weedbeds and other cover to stay out of sight, and flood water carrying rafts of weed that become draped on the angler's line like washing on a clothes line.

Low and Clear Water

The best way to deal with crystal-clear water is to fish at night, but that isn't always an option for many anglers, and not a few actually prefer to fish in daylight, in spite of it being much more difficult to contend with the conditions.

Many times the best answer is to choose deeper water with a good flow, and to pay particular attention to swims that lie in shade, beneath overhanging trees, for example. It's true, though, that whatever tackle and bait we use it will be very clearly seen by the fish. This, of course, has its advantages as well as its disadvantages, in that the fish will be able to find what we're offering them far more easily, and so we can appeal to their visual instincts far more than we normally can when the river is running with colour. For one thing it means that small baits can be seen from greater distances. For instance, maggot and caster trickling down the current is likely to be noticed by fish that are not swimming in that bait lane, simply because they can see it. So there is a chance, in that respect, that a constant trickle of bait through a swim will attract not only the fish that wander into the bait lane, but also those that swim close enough to see the bait going by. In a clear river 'close enough' can be several yards, as opposed to a few feet, or even less, in a high and coloured river.

ABOVE: *This pike had eyes bigger than its belly because it chased the barbel into the landing net and ended up getting landed itself.*

LEFT: *Even sizeable barbel occasionally bear the scars of attacks from pike.*

Of course, clear water is a real bonus to the roving angler who relies on spotting fish before he offers them a bait. When roving, make good use of the trees, bushes and vegetation along the banks, and give it the full Red Indian crawl up to the water's edge when you have to. You can learn so much about barbel feeding behaviour by just sitting or lying quietly and watching them as they browse the bottom, tasting and probing for morsels of food. Even better is when you can feed them with bait samples and watch how they react to these and feed on them – always bearing in mind, of course, that when you do the same thing with a rod in your hand, even though you still remain out of sight, they seem to know at times that 'the enemy' is at large! Observing barbel feeding in low and clear water will stand you in good stead when you *can't* see them, when the water is not so clear and you have to imagine what is happening along the bottom of the river.

The down side is that clear water means that the fish can also spot a predator more easily – and anything on the bank that moves and looks as if it doesn't belong there, such as an angler, and anything in the water that doesn't look natural and raises their suspicions to the point where they refuse to accept a bait, is treated as a predator. This includes the usual pike, of course.

Incidentally, Graham once caught a barbel of about 5lb that was chased straight into the landing net by a pike that was hardly any bigger!

Barbel, like most fish, are always on the alert for predators of all types, and it is not uncommon to catch barbel with predator wounds along their flanks. This means we have to do one, or both, of two things: camouflage ourselves and our tackle, or make the tackle less obvious.

Camouflage for the Angler
Although dull and sombre shades of green, grey and black will help you to go unnoticed, many specialist anglers have now got themselves kitted out with full outfits of camouflage clothing, and although this may look absurd to some, it does give you a distinct advantage when fishing clear water. There are times when you can't fish a swim from behind cover, and it isn't always practical to lie down and out of sight for the duration of a session, which is always the best option, so blending in with the background makes a lot of sense.

The background in most instances consists of trees, bushes and other undergrowth, and there is no doubt that the Realtree camouflage patterns match those better than anything else. On high banks, where there is no undergrowth, there may be a case for clothing that matches

John Searl uses this tree and foliage to blend into his surroundings.

the sky, usually pale blue or grey. So an angler wearing good quality camouflage clothing, providing he doesn't stand up and wave his arms around, will still be more acceptable than an angler wearing fluorescent orange. Unfortunately, however, in spite of several generations of anglers writing about wearing subtle clothing when fishing, the bright and gaudy, colourfully clothed, fish-scaring angling contingent can be seen every week.

Camouflage for the Tackle

Starting with the rod and reel, these are best with a matt finish so they don't reflect flashes of light into the clear water on each cast and retrieve. If you have a rod with a high gloss finish, then give it a rub with wire wool and take the shine off it. Don't overdo it, and you'll still retain the protective varnish; not that it's needed these days on carbon rods, except on the whippings, which are usually resin-coated anyway. Too many reels these days are made with highly polished parts and high gloss bodies, both of which mirror bright light into the water. Fortunately there are still some good reels made with dull and non-reflective materials for the body, and these are best for stalking wary fish in clear water.

There are two ways the line can be made less noticeable. One is to choose a line colour that blends with the bottom of the river, or at least the swim being fished: dark lines for over silt, light brown lines for over sand and gravel, green lines for in weed. But if we're going to follow that route, then we have to make sure the line is pinned to the bottom and not hung in mid-water or thereabouts like a washing line, and this means using a back lead, which is a good idea anyway in many river swims even when the water is coloured. A flying back lead, even at very short range, pins the line down a good two feet back from the end tackle.

The second way is to use a clear line, which – in theory at least – will show the colour of whatever bottom it's lying on or close to. You can take the precaution of taking the stark gloss off the line by rubbing it with damp, fine soil. Better still is to give it a good rub with the fly fisher's Fuller's Earth that will not only take the shine off the line, but help it sink, too.

Objects of similar size and shape as hooks lie on riverbeds in abundance, so although it is unlikely the hook will scare fish (the sight of it, not the feel of it) it is still best to avoid shiny silver and gold hooks, and to use those with a matt finish in grey, such as the Korum Seamless.

Dull baits such as these halibut pellets blend in on the riverbed, but barbel have little difficulty in finding them.

Weights and feeders are overlooked by too many anglers as potential fish-scaring items. It is best to use leads that have been coated to match the bottom, and there are some around these days that look like stones – in fact some, known as Stonze weights, either in lines or with a swivel, really are stones, and you can't get more natural than that. As for round plastic cylinders with holes in them, namely swimfeeders, these must be as far from being natural as you can get, but at least use green or brown ones, and whatever you use, couple it with a good long hook link to create a 'safe' distance between bait and lead/feeder.

Baits and Baiting

A particle bait such as maggot or caster, used in combination with hemp, will often work in clear water when big baits are ignored. Particle baits trickled through a swim are much less likely to arouse suspicion than a great lump of luncheon meat bouncing through or lying there starkly pink and obvious. When fishing clear water, the best bigger baits are boilies, pellets and pastes of a subtle, dull colour ranging through various shades of brown. Of course, none of this means that brightly coloured boilies, pink luncheon meat and bright yellow sweetcorn won't work at all, just that subtle colours may not deter that particularly wary big fish, for which normally you have to wait until dark to stand a chance of tempting.

Feeding the swim is best done before you actually fish, preferably with a mixture of particles such as hempseed, caster and pellet. Where possible they should be fed with a bait dropper an hour or so before you introduce a hookbait. Baiting and then leaving a swim while the fish move in and begin to feed confidently is always a good idea, whatever the colour of the water.

When this is not feasible, due to time restraints or the possibility of someone jumping the swim while you wait for it to mature, be very careful how you feed. Again, a particle approach – just trickling bait in without causing a great deal of disturbance – is probably best. Alternatively, when fishing a swim near the bank, try wrapping some Method mix, made from something like soaked pellets and crumbled boilies, around a camouflaged lead, and lower this into the swim. When the mix breaks down you're left with a very subtle rig that is least likely to spook the fish.

So just because you can't, or don't want to fish at night, don't think it's a waste of time fishing in daylight when the rivers run clear, because there's a great deal that can be done to ensure you get a fish or two. It all comes down to keeping a low profile with everything: yourself, your tackle and your bait.

High and Coloured Water

Given all the problems associated with fishing in floodwater – finding the fish, personal safety, finding a method that will work, and the extra strains on the gear – it is a wonder than anyone aside from the most fanatical barbel angler would bother. But when it comes to barbel and floodwater, we have conditions that suit the species perfectly. Barbel that had previously been torpid in clear winter conditions suddenly become active, utilizing their excellent senses of smell and taste to find food. The powerful currents of extra water hardly trouble the streamlined barbel, and in summer and winter alike, floodwater conditions can mean excellent sport on an otherwise dour river. Take all of this into consideration and it is hardly surprising that many keen barbel anglers relish a river in spate. But to get the best out of them it is important to have the right approach, beginning with personal safety, and only then paying attention to the other special aspects of this tough, challenging yet potentially rewarding aspect of barbel angling. What long experience does tell us is that barbel have no problems at all in the strongest of flood currents.

Indeed, barbel love extra water, especially in winter when it's accompanied by extra warmth. In most winters the level will generally be well above the usual summer level, which is why river level readings by the relevant authorities refer to 'normal summer level' and 'normal winter level'. So once the barbel have got through the transitional period of late autumn and early winter and settled to 'normal winter level', it no longer becomes significant until that

ABOVE: *A big Wye flood is a daunting prospect, and it may be safer not to venture on to its banks. Take extra care if you do.*

LEFT: *A small river flood is an ideal chance to catch barbel, provided it is safe to get on to the banks.*

level increases by several feet. That's when you have to look at the river through new eyes.

It's often been written that high water levels and the speed of the current should not deter you from fishing the usual barbel swims, that you should increase the weight of your bomb or feeder and get out there. And there is no argument with that, as barbel definitely do frequent the same swims that were 3ft deep in summer and could now be 10ft deep or more during a winter flood. Also, experienced river anglers know that the appearance of the surface water is not necessarily a good indication of what the current is like along the river bed, and that this deception can be even more pronounced during times of floodwater.

Graham remembers when he first discovered that barbel don't necessarily move out of their regular haunts to slack water when a river floods; sometimes they do and sometimes they don't, and part of the problem is, as always, finding them. He found this out on the River Dove. Graham takes up the story:

I'd caught plenty of fish over the years in flood-water conditions, but only in ideal floodwater conditions, when the river was on the first rise, which is when fish tend to get their bibs on, and

when the river was fining down following a flood, the time when the floodwater debris had been swept away. Those in-between times, when the river had reached a peak and raced though at an ever-increasing rate of knots, saw me behind a carp, tench or bream rod in summer, or a pike rod in winter, on a lake or mere. When I'd fished the river at the ideal times it had been either in slacks or slow glides where the pace was reasonable or nonexistent.

Then one particularly wet winter, at a time when my friend Dave Colclough and I were continually fishing for barbel and little else, it became a case of fish the rivers in far less than ideal conditions or not fish them at all, which was what led to us discovering that fishing floodwater is not half as difficult as we, and many others, imagine. Another thing that became apparent was that in some of the swims where you expected to use ¼lb or more of lead it actually needed considerably less. The surface suggested that, in some cases, the current would be too much to enable you to fish at all. But no, where you thought 6oz of lead would not have held bottom, as little as 1oz was easily sufficient. And this was over smooth gravel runs that should be the same pace from surface to bottom. Perhaps they were. Perhaps the look of

Dave Colclough holds the stamp of fish likely to show in flood conditions – be prepared for the bigger ones.

the surface was deceiving, but they certainly looked much faster to me than many of the swims that demanded several more ounces of lead. Don't expect that in every swim though, for in most you will need as much weight as the look of the current suggests, and especially when lots of debris is being carried down with the flow. Trial and error is the watchword.

Many of the swims where we caught fish were not the smooth glides you normally look for. Many times they were savage, boiling turmoils that at any other time I would have walked past without a second glance. We discovered that one such swim was fishable quite by accident.

It was on the Dove, at the tail end of a raging winter flood that had seen the river running down the main street of the village and swamping the Post Office. When we went out to fish, the river had dropped back, though was still about six feet over normal level. We headed for the slackest water we could find, and there was only one swim that appeared to give us a chance of wetting a line, and we had to fish almost side by side in the same piece of water. Right at the edge the river ran back on itself, slow enough to allow us to fish it with 1½oz leads. The temperature was just about mild enough to prompt barbel into feeding. Out went two heavily flavoured chunks of meat, and we sat back prepared to wait a long time for a bite. In other words, our confidence was not exactly soaring, and in the next two hours we never had a touch and debated the wisdom of being there.

And then a fish slid out of the water – no, not slid, it sprang out, and returned with a loud splash, much louder than the tumbling water of the river that was a constant roar in our ears. We didn't know what species it was, for it happened so quickly we saw only a shadow of it as it disappeared beneath the surface. What did take us completely by surprise was the fact that the fish had appeared right smack bang in the middle of the river where the current was like the Zambezi on a bad day. We couldn't believe our own eyes for a spell – at least not until it happened again a few minutes later, in the same spot.

Luckily we were positioned just right to fish the spot where the fish had appeared, which was just upstream of us. Upstream legering meant that the rod tip would spring back as soon as the

lead was dislodged when a fish picked up the bait. So the rods were propped almost at full height and a 4oz lead clipped on in place of the 1½s. They held bottom all right, even with the tips bent a few inches into them, and we sat back to await events. Normally we would be holding the rods ready to respond to bites, but in spite of seeing two fish (or the same fish twice) break surface, our confidence was still at a low ebb.

Which was a mistake, because Dave's rod tip sprang back like a startled cat. He picked up the rod but it was too late and he missed it. Within a minute or so my rod took on life, but I had the benefit of Dave's missed bite, was prepared for it and had the rod in my hand when the bait was picked up. The first barbel hit the net a minute or two later. This was the first of seven or eight we caught that day from that fast, racing water. We went home with snow swirling into our faces, faces that had grins to match the Cheshire Cat. Not because of the fish we'd caught, welcome as they were, but because now we knew the river was fishable, and that fish would feed in conditions we had previously avoided like the plague.

New Swims
What you should never forget, and this is equally important when choosing winter barbel swims, is that when the water has risen several feet, new barbel swims are created. For example, gravel patches that were exposed to the elements throughout most of the summer are now covered with several feet of flowing water, marginal vegetation, trees and bushes become submerged, and pools form where previously no pools had existed. Back eddies are created in places that were dry just a few weeks before, and creases form in smooth glides that previously had no crease.

And remember, too, that some of those newly created swims will be untapped areas of food, because previously they were either dry or just too shallow for the barbel to forage them. There is no doubt that when formerly dry land is covered with water of sufficient depth (and that need be no more than a couple of feet) it will be exploited by fish, and particularly by barbel that are experts at finding newly exposed larders of

ABOVE: *This gravel is usually under a foot of water even in normal summer conditions, but prolonged drought has left it dry.*

BELOW: *The river is well up and coloured, but it's warm and there's a good chance of a big barbel in this known holding spot.*

natural food. Marginal swims are at their best when the first flood covers previously dry land, and this is when the barbel begin to exploit them. Only later, when the recently flooded margin swims have been covered for several days, do the old haunts, in the thick of the flood, come into their own.

Where flooded margin swims are concerned, don't make the mistake that many anglers do, of only looking for big, obvious swims. Those pools and back eddies don't have to be a score of square yards or more to attract barbel. Some favourite floodwater swims are no more than a single square yard of quiet water lying close to the bank with a crease separating them from a raging current. If you walk along the river and look carefully at the margins you'll find several of these tiny pools and back eddies, and one or more of them will be a favourite larder for barbel. Barbel seem to be just as inclined to frequent these newly formed little swims in winter as they are in summer, probably because they offer respite from heavy currents, and even barbel must be glad of them at times when they've been fighting the current for some considerable while.

To give you a better idea of just how close to the bank some winter floodwater swims are, they are so close they can't be fished unless you're about six feet back from the edge. Yes, it is sometimes possible to go upriver a few yards and drop a bait in from there, but by far the best option is to sit back from the water's edge and just lower the end tackle and bait straight down from the rod tip. You can get this off to a fine art by setting up two rod rests so that the rod is held at an angle of about 45 degrees. Push the rod forwards on the rests until the tip, with the baited end tackle dangling below, is directly over the exact spot where you want the bait to enter the water. Then back wind the reel very slowly until the line falls slack as the tackle finds the bottom. Then lift the rod off the front rod rest and drop it into another front rod rest planted about a yard to the upstream side.

Of course, the positioning of the rod rests has all been worked out on arrival at the water, or previously if fishing a known swim, so that while you are actually fishing there is never any need to approach the water's edge and risk spooking

any fish that could be feeding right under your feet. Many times you will get a distinct warning of a pending bite, for the rod tip will quiver a little, or nod a few times as the barbel pokes around. Be ready. Even so, in such swims it pays to use a reel with a free-spool facility, and make sure this is set when waiting for a bite. Bites can come out of the blue, and the first thing you'll know about it is when the rod does a sudden nosedive for the river. If there wasn't a free-spool facility involved it could mean a lost rod (or a broken line) because you have only to take your hand off the rod and look away from it for a single second for it to happen when fishing such a short line. The free-spool allows the fish to take off in safety, and you can then grab the rod, disengage the free-spool, and walk downstream so that you can play and land the fish well away from the swim, leaving it relatively undisturbed and ready for another bait.

Graham has had half a dozen big fish in a four or five hour session from such tiny swims, mainly due to the one little spot being so attractive to them; an oasis in a desert. And also because the swim was never corrupted, because he took the precaution of walking downstream for twenty yards or so before giving them enough stick to bring them in.

It is a good idea to have a really close look at good floodwater swims when the river is well back within its banks. That way you can pick out the detail, and can pinpoint exactly where your bait will do most good, you will know exactly where any snags are, and precisely where to position the rod rests so that the bait can be lowered and presented with pinpoint accuracy. And most important, taking stock of the swim at low water is essential for your personal safety.

Pay attention to this story of what happened to Graham one day as he recalls the first time he ever fished the lower Severn;

I'd been invited to fish the lower Severn by a couple of friends who, it appeared later, had assumed I had fished that part of the Severn before. I hadn't, and when I saw the river, which was in full flood, I didn't realize just how deep the swim was that I'd chosen. It was a massive flood, and to get to the river we'd tramped

Personal Safety on Flooded Rivers

Fishing any river in normal conditions has its dangers. Undercut and slippery banks, deep water and strong currents are all potentially dangerous should you take an unexpected dip into the river. But in flood conditions, where the normal river bank is under water, the water is much deeper and possibly colder than normal, the current is stronger, and finally the banks are extra slippery or damaged, all make for much more dangerous conditions where extra care is required. Put your personal safety first, second and last. Don't risk trying to inch across flooded sections of bank when you are not sure where the edge is, or which may be dangerously undercut by the floodwater. Consider whether there is a real danger of sliding in, possibly into twelve feet of icy water, because the bank side is so slippery that you can hardly stand up, never mind when you want to land or return a barbel. Consider your footwear regarding grip, and consider using a safety rope or even a buoyancy aid.

Watch out, too, on rising rivers. Some rivers, especially those with steep valleys that drain impervious clay or rock, can rise at an alarming rate after very heavy rain. The fact that the river is already high and the ground waterlogged makes the possibility of a flood surge even more likely. On some rivers, where the water is already across the fields, there is the possibility of finding yourself cut off from higher ground by rising water. Take great care if local access roads or lanes are under water: it is often safest to pull on your waders and check the depth in front of the car with a landing net before attempting to drive across. Drive into too deep water and you may find your car floating, with the water flooding in, and the risk of water getting into the air intake (a blown engine!).

When a river is this high you may not be able to drive through adjacent roads.

across fields that had mini lakes almost everywhere. The river level had begun to recede, as could be seen clearly by the floodline of debris, and was now, so I thought, just about at the top of its banks. The water was still for several yards before it reached the torrent that was racing through. When I cast the 5oz lead into the current it seemed to take forever to reach bottom and I estimated the swim was about twenty-five feet deep, and the line was almost vertical.

I sat some three feet back from the water's edge. The first savage bite from a barbel was not long after I'd cast in, and it took me by surprise. I was adjusting the rear legs of my chair, and I automatically lunged for the rod and grabbed it. At the same time my right foot slid across the greasy bank and my leg disappeared into the river, right up to my crotch. With my left hand clawing at the bank to stop me from sliding any further in, and my right hand hanging on to the rod, with the reel screaming as the barbel took

off for the Bristol Channel, and me screaming at deaf ears for help, I eventually clawed my way up the bank far enough to grasp my bank stick and haul myself back to relative safety. I landed the barbel, a fish of about 8lb, whinged to myself about my wet leg, and thought no more about it.

That is, until I made another visit some few weeks later, when the river was back to normal winter level. I went to the same swim, and only then realized just how close I'd been to losing my life. Where I'd been sat was well back from the true edge of the river and my line had been snaking its way through a number of bushes down the steep bank to end up in the edge of the real river bank. If I'd lost my grip on the bank I would have slid down a dozen feet or so and finished up in the raging torrent, with no chance of survival.

It frightens me to this day to think about how close I'd come to a watery grave. And I still marvel at how I managed to land that barbel without once becoming snagged up.

A big Stour flood has put at least three feet of dirty water over the fields; that's the tops of the fence posts!

A small lift like this Dorset Stour summer flood can sometimes trigger jaded barbel into feeding well.

Of course, the moral of the story is: don't be like Graham at that time, and check out the lie of the land and the river when the water is low. Floodwater can be great for barbel fishing, but no fish is worth risking your life for.

Tackle for Floodwater

There's floodwater and floodwater. There's floodwater that makes little rivers go a shade darker in colour and up a foot or two in level. And there's serious floodwater that makes big rivers change to the colour of strong tea and rise by several feet. Although some quite significant changes in tackle are required for big rivers in serious flood, the changes required for small rivers is usually only an increase in the weight of the feeder or bomb.

Rods

In heavy floods you often need a heavier rod, because your usual rod may be bent over by the force of the current to the point where a bite can only be indicated by the butt lifting off the ground! You also need a heavier rod for casting the huge weights that are necessary – as much as 8oz in the worst floods on the biggest rivers, though generally 5oz is the most you'll need. Don't even consider a quivertip unless you're fishing slack pools in the margins, and even then they're usually unnecessary. Long rods up to 13ft are often best, because you will need to set the rod as high as you reasonably can to keep as much line out of the water as possible, for the more line there is in the water, the more pressure can be applied to it by the current, all of which pulls the end tackle and bait out of position. Take a look at the range of carp rods in the $1\frac{3}{4}$lb to 2lb class.

Reels

If you normally prefer to use reels in the smaller sizes, then you need to shift up a size or two, mainly to match the heavier rods that are necessary. Free-spool reels are best, as the free-spool facility can be set to just hold in the current, but will give line when a barbel takes the bait. Reels in the 5000 class are ideal.

Lines

The weight we're casting dictates the line,

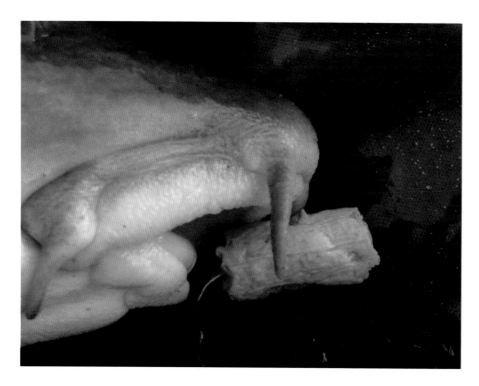

A big chunk of smelly sausage is ideal for catching floodwater barbel.

because continually casting extremely heavy weights puts a great deal of strain on all the tackle, but especially the line. The down side of this is that we need to keep the line diameter at a minimum, as the greater the diameter, the greater the pressure the current can exert on it. This is when a low diameter/high strength braided line comes into its own. A line, braid or mono, of 12lb bs is minimum for this job. Any colour of line will do, as the opacity of the water eliminates the necessity to camouflage it.

Weights
Obviously the bomb or feeder needs to be stepped up by several ounces so that it holds bottom. In the case of a swimfeeder, it needs to be heavy enough to hold bottom when it's emptied as we don't want it rolling out of the feed lane and presenting the hookbait elsewhere. The best leads for gripping the bottom are known as watch leads, which are very popular with sea anglers, but coarse tackle manufacturers make pear-shaped watch leads known as gripper leads. Unlike watch leads, these are coated to keep them discreet on the bottom; although camouflaging weights and feeders is

nowhere near as essential in coloured water, it still pays to be careful not to use anything shiny and obvious.

Baits for Floodwater
Realistically, you don't need anything different from the baits you use in normal river levels if you're fishing with the same approach – that is, with a swimfeeder or PVA bag to create a bait lane. Large lobworms can be excellent, although it must be said that lobs can be a hit-and-miss bait in that they seem to be great barbel catchers on some rivers but not others, even in floodwater. It is wise to consider the possibility that the swim you're fishing may have such a fast flow along the bottom any feed you attach to the end tackle, whether it's via a swimfeeder or a PVA bag, may be flushed away so fast it's a waste of time doing it in the first place. Hence the reason why so many regular floodwater anglers don't feed at all, but instead use a large, smelly bait, something like a heavily flavoured boilie or pellet, or a chunk of peperami or flavoured luncheon meat.

There is much to be said for this approach, as it is highly likely the barbel will be relying more on their sense of smell to find food in heavy floodwater conditions than on any of their other means of finding food, so a larger than usual, single hookbait makes a lot of sense. Fishing a single hookbait also means you can safely cast to various areas of the swim, searching for barbel, without any fear of spreading loose feed across the river, which is never a good idea.

Flavours and Dips

If you follow the single hookbait approach it is best to flavour the bait in a dip for several days before fishing, so that the flavour is soaked well into the bait and not just on the surface, which can wash off very fast indeed in a heavy flow – unless of course you make your own boilies, when you can build this extra flavour into the base mix. But don't dispense with bait dips, as you can still give your bait some extra initial impact by dipping the bait before casting or, as some barbel anglers do, by having several baited hook lengths soaking in a bait dip as they fish.

The end tackle should incorporate a quick-change method so that a new and well soaked bait can be clipped on for every cast.

Confidence

Confidence is the key word to all successful fishing, but it is the *main* ingredient when it comes to fishing floodwater. If you've never fished a raging, flooded river before, then you need to break through that barrier that prevents so many anglers from having the confidence to do so. Cast to areas of a flooded river that look impossible to fish, if those areas usually hold barbel in conditions of normal level. Look for the quieter swims when such swims seem more likely. But whatever you do, go for it positively and with determination, because when you break through the mental barrier that tells you that fishing a flooded river is a waste of time, and fish one of those days when the barbel are really 'having it', you'll never look back.

Graham caught this River Dove fourteen-pounder in flood conditions.

11 FLOAT FISHING

The Approach

Resolve to Float Fish

It's all too easy to fall into the trap of believing that barbel fishing has to be about legering, and having fallen into that trap, to plan your trips around legering tactics. Like most specialist anglers, if you tend to arrive at the riverbank an hour or so before dark and continue fishing into the night for a few hours, then float fishing is a non starter because there simply isn't enough daylight time to make float fishing an option. Instead, try to arrive earlier, or shift your barbel fishing to the morning rather than the evening. It's not the way to go if your priority is to catch the biggest fish, because for this, legering into darkness usually has the edge. If, however, enjoying the method you use to catch the fish is all-important, then delivering that float through a swim and seeing it go under to the pull of a barbel, and playing such a fish on a stepped-up float rod, should definitely be top of your list.

Stick or Waggler Float?

When thinking of float fishing for barbel, most river anglers err towards a stick float or Avon type, which attach at both top and bottom. They will seek out swims that lend themselves to such floats – swims along their own bank, or no more than a yard or two beyond that. Generally this is the best approach. But on some rivers where there are swims further out, there is a deadly waggler method that will increase the number of swims that can be tackled successfully beyond the range of a stick or an Avon. Rather than select the swim to suit the float-fishing method you'd like to fish, instead choose swims on the

Mark piles on the pressure to a lively Avon fish at the end of the season.

This selection of floats suitable for barbel fishing includes balsa floats, goose quill Avons, a plastic Chubber and a thick peacock waggler – all these take a hefty shot load.

basis of their fish-holding potential, and then choose a float type accordingly.

The thing to remember when choosing a method (float or leger) is that there is little point in using a float if you're targeting the occasional individual fish. Float fishing on rivers is for those swims where a shoal resides. This can be a big shoal of four-pounders, or a small group of half a dozen or so eight-pounders or larger, but anything less does not fit into the usual concept of float fishing. This is to create an active feeding area where the fish are taking bait 'on the run', rather than seeking out baits that lie on, or trundle along the bottom. Of course, there are times when it is easier to deliver a float-fished bait to a big individual fish than it is to deliver the bait on leger tackle, but let's put to one side the exceptions and discuss the general concept of float fishing.

The Advantage of Float Fishing

The big advantage of float fishing is that it keeps the angler active, and an active angler is a thinking angler. You'd think it would be the other way round, that an angler who is legering with a static bait would have the time to sit and think while he's waiting for a bite. But this is not so, and it is the float angler who is picturing his swim all the time he's fishing; every little pull-under, duck and dive of the float is building up

Small barbel such as this two-pounder held by Stu Dexter are great fun to catch on float tackle.

This float-caught barbel fell to waggler tactics.

that picture. All the time he is assessing the amount of bait he's loose feeding into the swim, not just the amount but the regularity of it, continually adjusting according to the response, or not, that he's getting from the fish. The float angler has more options when it comes to both major and minor tackle adjustments and can deliver his bait through the swim in a much wider variety of ways.

The down side of float fishing is that it usually demands lighter tackle: softer rods, finer lines and smaller hooks, which isn't exactly what you want when barbel fishing. However, the reality is that these authors have caught a lot of barbel on the float, usually using 5lb to 6lb hook lengths and sizes 18 to 14 hooks, and not lost any more fish than when legering with heavier tackle. What happens is that when you've got the beefier legering tackle, you tend to use it, and therefore the fish react accordingly by fighting more tenaciously. When float fishing you have to take a much more softly, softly approach to playing them, countering the barbel's efforts to escape with measures more akin to subtle persuasion than uncompromising heaving.

But what about the snags, you might ask. What use is a 6lb line when an 8lb or bigger barbel is charging for those sunken branches or tree roots?

The first thing to remember is that you don't float fish too close to snags, or the barbel will be in them as soon as you strike the hook home. Fish a reasonable distance from the snags, though, and whereas on heavy leger gear they will still attempt to hurtle towards them, on float gear they don't seem to charge off when they're not having their heads pulled off. While you don't allow them to have all their own way, you certainly don't try to bully them. What's the point when you don't have the fire power? No, the answer is to keep the line tight and steer them, sometimes with a pull away from the snags, sometimes with a pull towards them. And there's not much more to tell you than that, for what you have to do is react to what they do, and what that reaction should be can only be judged at the time. Certainly they'll take off at times, and all you can do is hang on and hope, but most often they'll behave as though they don't know what's happening to them, and if you don't bend the rod into them unduly it's best to keep them in a state of ignorance and persuade, rather than coerce, them into submission.

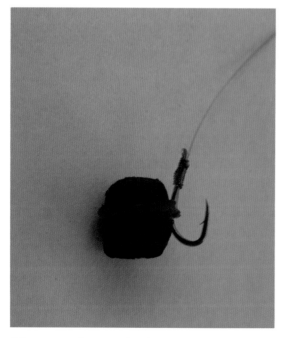

It's easy enough to use a bait band to attach an 8mm pellet to a strong, forged size 12 hook for float fishing for barbel.

Baits

The decision to float fish ties in nicely with the fact that daylight fishing for barbel usually means that fishing with particle baits is an excellent option, especially when the water is low and clear. Bigger meat, paste, boilie and pellet baits are fine for legering on bigger hooks when there is colour in the water and when it goes dark. But particle baits, especially maggots, casters and hemp, are the ideal float-fishing bait, with casters the best choice, followed by maggots (if the minnows are not too plentiful and suicidal), then sweetcorn and small pellets.

Why Not Have a Go?

So why not do something different yourself this season, and give float fishing for barbel a go? Do you have to sit and leger every time you fish the river? Or wander the river with a leger rod? Do you have to have the best chance of catching a double to enjoy a session? Do you have to fish into darkness? You don't *have* to do any of those things. And if you've never had a barbel on float gear, you don't know what you're missing. It's barbel fishing with the emphasis on fun!

Float-Fishing Tackle

Although mainstream barbel gear is covered in Chapters 5 and 6, the gear for float fishing is sufficiently specialized to be discussed separately.

Rods

There are several options for a float-fishing rod, but whichever one we choose it must be well suited to lines between 5lb and 8lb. Standard match rods, although versatile enough to use 5lb line at a pinch, don't really have enough 'grunt' to tackle this style of fishing. It is far better to choose what are usually described as 'power' match (occasionally as 'tench' float) rods. These rods are designed for 5–8lb lines, and should be light enough to hold comfortably during several hours of hard trotting. A standard 13ft rod is ideal, although you may find the power match rods in a slightly shorter length of 12ft 6in or 12ft 9in.

Beware of rods that have heavy loading in the

butt to counteract a top-heavy rod, or that feel top-heavy. While rods like this are all right for static float fishing on a lake, you may find them hard work on a fast river. There are two alternatives to power match rods. One is to use a standard Avon rod (with its Avon top, not the quiver tops) with a test curve of 1.25lb. Most such rods are 12ft in length, and there are some very good ones. Again, as with the match rods they must be light and well balanced, and have an action sufficiently 'crisp', or not floppy, to make float fishing viable.

There has been a new development in recent years of 'pellet waggler' rods that are usually 11ft, though sometimes longer. These rods are intended for fishing with short, stumpy waggler floats on heavily stocked commercial carp fisheries using 6–8lb line, targeting carp from 5–14lb. It is apparent that the better, lighter and longer versions ought to make ideal barbel float rods; they will certainly have a good 'playing' action. If you are looking for a new rod, have a good look at all the options; try them with a reel fitted, threading the line through the rings so you can see how they bend under load, and how well balanced they feel.

Reels
There are two options for a good trotting reel for barbel. The fashionable one is a quality centrepin, though the alternative, a small to medium sized, well designed fixed spool reel, is equally effective. It comes down to personal preference rather than any perceived advantages. Both will do the job well, and each has its advocates. It is better to concern yourself with the factors that matter when trotting, which is feeding and bait presentation, rather than get too involved on the superiority of one reel over the other. Just go with the type of reel that you fish with best and are most comfortable with.

Centrepin reels, used in a legering situation, were mentioned in Chapter 5, but for trotting the requirements are slightly more specialized. A good trotting reel should be free running and lightweight. A good-sized spool helps to retrieve line more quickly at the end of each trot, but other than that it's a case of looking at the reels on the market and choosing one that suits your

This reel is a little on the large size for trotting, as Mark is struggling to reach the spool lip easily.

style and budget. With good trotting centre-pins costing from £50 up to £300 and more, it is all too easy to be seduced by some wonderful works of engineering: but it's your money, so if you choose to spoil yourself, then why not?

The ideal fixed spool reel for trotting should be lightweight, not too big – a 2500 size is ideal – with a good drag, and made with a spool that is in easy reach of your forefinger when you hold the rod. Both Daiwa and Shimano make very

This 2500-sized fixed spool reel is perfect for float fishing for barbel.

good reels of this type, and generally you get what you pay for. The more expensive reels are smoother, have better drags, and will probably last longer in the long term. As you will be using a line with a maximum breaking strain of 8lb, the small size of the reel doesn't matter too much. Load spools with 6lb and 8lb line and you have a wide choice for float fishing and light legering.

Lines for Trotting

The ideal line for trotting should float easily, and be robust yet controllable. For many anglers, bulk spools of Daiwa Sensor fit the bill at around £7 for a bulk spool that can be a mile or more of line. It floats well, is tough and behaves well, and at such a cheap price you can afford to replace the last 100 yards on your reel regularly. Other lines with similar qualities will also be suitable. One thing to remember about Sensor is that the breaking strains are under-rated; this means that 4lb line actually breaks at

a wet knotted strength of over 6lb, the 6lb at over 8lb, and so on. This explains why it seems a little thick for its breaking strain as compared to other more accurately measured lines. On a centrepin for trotting you may find 100 yards/metres too much as it tends to bed in, so it may be better to have a lesser amount, such as 70 yards, though always allow for your longest trot, plus enough to cater for a fish reaching a long way downstream with you unable to follow.

Although it is possible to use braid for float fishing, the complete lack of stretch makes it unforgiving when playing barbel. The shock absorption quality of regular nylon is your secret weapon in soaking up the fight, and this will allow you to beat a barbel quickly and effectively when barbel fishing, despite using lighter tackle than conventional leger tackle.

Floats

Your float requirements will depend largely on the waters that you fish. Standard trotting patterns such as Avon-style floats, balsas and, to a lesser extent, stick floats all have their uses. The style of trotting for barbel has great emphasis on dragging the bait along the riverbed, which means using plenty of weight well down in your shotting pattern. Tackling the same swim for chub or dace, for instance, would require much lighter shotting patterns. This means seeking out the heavier end of the float ranges. If, for instance, a float type is available in the range 3AAA to 7AAA then it is the 5AAA to 7AAA ones that you are interested in. Think of it like this; weigh up the swim along its total length, and then consider what the minimum weight of float load would be to allow you to dominate it – to have full control over your float throughout the entire length of the swim. And then for trotting for barbel, double or treble it. This will nail down the bait so that it trundles slowly along the bottom without fluttering up, which is what would happen if you used light shotting. Light shotting is fine for chub, indeed a great advantage, but of little use for barbel.

Avon-type floats, especially ones with thick goose-quill tips, are ideal for barbel fishing. The biggest problem is obtaining them. Mark has been float making for as long as he has been fishing so has no trouble making his own to any specification, and for Avons that includes crow quill, goose quill and swan quill-based designs. These floats certainly ride the water much better (and cast well, too) than plastic versions of Avon floats. Drennan and others make 'Chubber'-style floats from clear plastic with hefty shot-carrying capacity, and some of

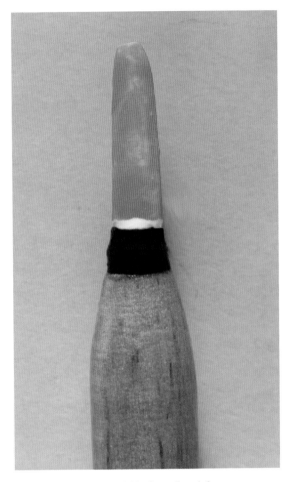

ABOVE: The thick tip of this Avon float is buoyant enough to cope with boily water.

BELOW: Although designed for float fishing on stillwaters, these so-called 'pellet wagglers' can be successfully pressed into service for float fishing shallow, rugged waters for barbel.

these in the larger sizes are a 'must' for the barbel float angler.

It is worth learning to make your own floats: balsa wood is easy enough to obtain, as are goose quills. The other things you need are the tools – a fine hacksaw, modelling knife, some small sharp drills and fine paintbrushes – and other materials such as good quality yacht varnish, matt white and fluorescent red paint, Araldite or balsa cement and some fine whipping thread. Then it's just a case of trying – and often failing – to make some floats. Style your floats on existing floats at first to get some idea of the correct proportions, but as you gain experience you can develop your own designs.

You may have more luck with standard balsa floats and the larger sizes of stick floats that are still around. Paul Woodward of 'Woodies' Tackle in Hereford manufactures a range of specialist floats for fishing this style of fishing on big and rugged rivers – they're designed for the Wye – and you may find them obtainable through your local tackle shop.

A selection of suitable hooks, split shot, plummets and large olivettes, plus a large disgorger: all useful for float fishing.

The best type of trotting float for this style of fishing has a 'shoulder' below the tip, which enables you to hold back better than with a float that doesn't have it.

Anglers don't normally associate waggler fishing with barbel fishing, but it is a successful option on the right waters. What does change from standard waggler fishing is the type of waggler used. Standard waggler floats are slim and may have thinner inserts to make them more sensitive: we need the opposite for barbel fishing because the objective is to fish well over-depth, dragging the bait along the bottom, so the type of waggler required is extremely buoyant. This means a much thicker waggler than normal. Peacock wagglers made from really thick quill are ideal, and you want one at least 10in (25cm) long so that it can be undershotted with 3–4in (7.5–10cm) sticking out of the water when you fish it. Another viable option is to use the bigger sizes of the modern thick balsa dowel 'pellet' wagglers, or to make your own from balsa dowel. In both cases, floats that take a minimum shot load of 3–4 SSG shot are ideal.

Shots and Weights

A good selection of Anchor double-cut shot plus some No. 8 shot should meet nearly all your float-fishing needs. An added refinement is to use large tungsten olivette weights (3–8g) instead of a bulk of several large shots; you will find that the streamlined shape and extra density helps to keep the bait well down better than modern tin-based shot in the larger sizes. A modern alternative to shot, or rather an addition to the shot you normally use, is Kryston's Heavy Metal tungsten putty. This can be moulded around shot for additional weight, or around the knots on the loops that join hook length to main line, or an elongated piece of it moulded along part of the hook link. There are many ways you can use tungsten putty to vary your presentation, and it's always worth carrying a tub.

Hooks

Because we match the hook to both the bait being used and the job in hand we need small hooks (sizes 16 to 12) that are strong for their

size to match the line that we will be tying them to – even the smaller hooks are tied to 6lb line, and the bigger ones to 7lb. A typical well tried hook for this style of fishing is the Drennan Super Specialist. It makes a good choice for its qualities of a thicker wire than normal, incurved point, forging (slightly flattened wire to increase strength) and quality steel.

Bait Droppers and Other Accessories

Apart from other accessories already covered in Chapter 6, there are several bits and pieces also useful for float fishing. To help your line to float, a tin of Mucilin line floatant is useful as is a floating line spray. One essential is a couple of good-sized hook-on plummets so that you can explore the depths of the swim. For feeding the swim a large-pouched catapult and large bait dropper are both essential. The final useful accessory is a bait stand for bait boxes, or alternatively a bait bag or apron that you can hang around your neck. Both are useful in helping to have bait close to hand so that you can loose feed the swim regularly without having to continually bend down.

To Sit, Stand or Wade?

While many barbel anglers sit on specialist chairs when legering, these are mainly too low to be much use when trotting. The alternatives are therefore to stand on the bank, to wade in the river, if practical, or to sit on something with more height than a low chair. There is no doubt that keeping your profile low can be advantageous, and that standing, whether on the bank or in the river is tiring, which just leaves sitting down. One straightforward way to achieve this is to use a lightweight plastic seat box to carry your gear and to sit on. Provided you don't fill it to the top with gear it will still be carryable, and with the addition of adjustable OctoPlus legs, you can level it too. Alternatively, you will have to find a lightweight chair that gives you an upright seating position.

Trotting

Selecting a Swim

Before setting out to catch barbel on the float it

This low seat is high enough to be all right for float fishing.

is vital to pick a suitable swim. Ideal conditions are a swim that is neither too deep nor too shallow. Less than 4ft of water is tricky to float fish in the way that we want to accomplish; not impossible, but tricky. A deep swim – say, over 8ft – is fishable, but is it likely to hold barbel? It will help if the bottom is clean sand or fine gravel rather than rocky. Holding barbel, preferably a good shoal of middleweights from 4–8lb, is the most important ingredient for a good swim.

We also need summer or early autumn conditions with the river in normal trim. Float fishing is hard work that can be rewarding provided there is a chance of a reward. It is essential to study your chosen swim for a few minutes when you arrive; take your time just looking. See how the current flows, where the weedbeds are, the position of any snags, how the wind is blowing, and whether you can get below a hooked fish if required. Avoid very snaggy swims; your gear hasn't got the 'grunt' to battle it out with a big

barbel in such circumstances, and consequently losing a succession of barbel because of this is irresponsible.

Watch out for strong facing or downstream winds. It is imperative to be able to control your float without the wind blowing it off line. Save such a swim for another calmer day, or tackle it with a legering approach.

On some rivers it is advantageous to get into the river by quietly wading so that you can get closer to the barbel and feed more accurately as well as control your gear better. Stealth is of the essence here, and it can pay to wade to a position where there is a weedbed immediately in front of you so that this provides cover. If you do wade, then a bait apron is essential so that you don't have to make repeated trips back to the bank.

Tackling Up

Choose your float with care: think heavy, much heavier than if you were tackling the same swim

Mark concentrates on his float on the Wye at Hereford.

for chub, roach or dace. You are looking to be able to inch the float through the swim with the float set over-depth. For standard top and bottom floats, use three float rubbers and put the bulk shot around 2ft (60cm) from the hook. Below this, put a dropper shot around 10in (25cm) from the hook. This shotting pattern is a starting point. You may wish to drag more line on the bottom at some stage, in which case it may be better not only to increase the depth that the float is set to, but also to move the bulk further from the hook. You may need to over-shot the float so that it will sink unless retarded during the trot.

Before over-shotting the float it is best to do the initial plumbing of the swim. You don't need to plumb every inch, but at least get a good idea of the depth, and try to find any depressions or rises in the riverbed. Having done so it is better to feel your way around the swim by gradually increasing the depth on the float a couple of inches at a time until even when held back hard it still drags under, and then take 2in (5cm) off.

Feeding

How you go about feeding the swim depends very much on its nature, but a well proven way is to start by introducing several bait-droppers full of mainly hemp with some casters and perhaps some small pellets (3mm or 4mm). From then on, feed a mixture of hemp, casters and small pellets at every cast. This regular feeding is vital, because it will often take an hour or two before the barbel switch on to feeding, and that's only going to happen if the feeding is continuous. This is why you need a lot of bait for a float-fishing session on a river. But by using a mixture of relatively cheap hemp and pellets to bulk out your casters (a truly great bait for barbel) you can reduce the cost considerably by only needing three pints of casters with similar quantities each of hemp and pellets.

When feeding a swim, make sure you know that the loose feed is getting down to the area of the swim that you want it to: if the bait is swept downstream over the heads of the barbel it will be wasted. Some good barbel trotting swims have thick weedbeds that stop at the head of the

swim. By feeding on top of the weed your bait filters down to the bottom without being washed away. You may need to feed upstream using a catapult to allow for the current. Don't be afraid of repriming the swim using the bait dropper to re-establish a bed of bait. Doing this too often is not advisable, however, due to the disturbance this entails.

Keep Control

Having firmly established a regular feeding regime, it is equally important to concentrate on trotting through your swim with as much skill as you can muster. Catching barbel on the float isn't like catching dace; bites will be relatively few and far between, yet on every trot you must expect a bite, and you will only get those bites if your bait presentation is spot on. That means plenty of patience, perseverance and the ability to keep putting that float through the swim skilfully while maintaining the regular heavy feeding.

It is important to keep close control of the float so that you are slowing its progress right through the trot – one of the advantages of skilful use of a centrepin reel. Generally, when trying to catch barbel this way you are trying to fish well over-depth while holding back as much as possible. You may have to add more shot to the bulk to stop the float from riding out of the water – over-shotting – but this is just part of the method. Watch out for awkward winds that spring up during the day; you may have to change the float to an even bigger one. Consider, too, whether to alter the exact line you are trotting from time to time, or to alter the depth both up and down, or even to move the bulk shots closer or further away from the hook.

Waggler Tactics

Waggler fishing for barbel is almost the opposite of conventional float fishing using a top and bottom trotting float. Instead of holding back to slow down the float, we drag a lot of line and shots on the bottom to slow it down. While two thirds of the shot load is placed around the float, the way in which the remainder is used varies according to the circumstances. A good starting point is to have a small bulk of three or four BB shot about 4ft (1m) from the hook. Below this, string out no. 8 shot at 6in (15cm) intervals. It is most of these small shot that will drag along the bottom depending on how much over-depth the float is set. Ensure that the overall shot load is less than the actual shot load so that the tip sticking out can help drag the rig through the swim. When this method is working well the waggler makes its way majestically downstream, bumping and dipping in a predictable rhythm until it rapidly buries from a barbel.

The amount of control you have over the float and line is limited, but provided you mend the line to keep the worst of any bow out of it, a long sweeping strike will pick up the line well enough to set the hook. Although you can use a centrepin for this method, it is easier to use a fixed spool.

Feeding is similar to standard trotting, especially regarding quantity and regularity, but due to increased range a catapult is likely to be essential. Using a bait dropper also becomes more difficult, though it is worth considering, just to lay down a bed of hemp.

To drag line on the bottom you need the very thickest of peacock wagglers, like this one.

The size of the Wye at Hereford is daunting to the float angler, but Mark has had some terrific barbel sport float fishing there.

12 CARE AND CONSERVATION

Caring for Barbel

Barbel, like most species, give thousands of anglers so much pleasure the least we can do is take care of them to the best of our ability. This isn't meant to be sentimental, but a recognition of the practical responsibility that all anglers owe to the fish they love to catch. Not only does the care and conservation of fish make us better anglers and better people, it goes a long way to ensuring that the generations of anglers that follow us will continue to enjoy fishing for them as much as we have.

Be Prepared

Before you even begin fishing you should have everything prepared and ready for when you hook a fish. The landing net should be within

easy reach, unless you are planning to land the fish away from your fishing position due to snags or an insecure bank. In that case the landing net should be placed in the landing area. The unhooking mat should be close to the landing site, as should unhooking gear, weigh sling and scales. Also, if you intend to photograph a notable fish the camera should be set so that it's on the right setting when you switch it on, remote control ready if you're using one, and a tripod or other camera-holding device set up ready to use, or as near ready as possible.

The idea is to do everything you can to make landing, unhooking, weighing, photographing and returning fish as quick and smooth an operation as possible. This is best for the fish and best for you: the quicker you get a fish back in the water following a recovery period, the

The scales were ready for this barbel as they were on the edge of the unhooking mat.

This barbel has been efficiently played and is coming to the net long before exhaustion.

quicker you'll be trying to catch another one. Take a leaf from the match angler's book: be ready and be efficient, a place for everything and everything in its place.

Playing Barbel

So what has playing barbel got to do with caring for barbel? A lot, in fact, because too many anglers fish too light for such a hard-fighting species, and then take too long to play them. This leads to them becoming totally exhausted and then the angler, thinking he's doing the right thing, holds the fish in the margins, waits for it to kick a little, and then releases it. If the fish is lucky it will manage to swim or sink to the bottom, remain in an upright position and survive the ordeal. A lucky fish will also go belly up close enough to the side for the angler to scoop it out again in his landing net and have another go at helping it to recover. An unlucky

fish will appear to swim away and then go belly up some way downstream where the current carries it to its doom. The angler, totally unaware of what's happened, goes home thinking he's caught and carefully returned a fine barbel that he did well to catch on such light tackle. The truth is that his too-light gear has caused the death of a fish, and possibly a big fish that fought for an extended period.

There is no need to fish light for barbel: they are not a particularly difficult species to catch when it comes to tackle and bait choice, not being especially shy of lines and hooks, and there is nothing sporting in 'giving them a chance'. You should always fish as heavy as you can within practical reason and land them as fast as possible. *You* play the fish, don't let *them* play you.

If you've done your homework correctly you'll know where any snags lie both in and around the vicinity of the swim, and therefore you'll know when to apply more pressure to stop a fish getting into them. It's important that you know the swim before hooking a barbel because it could well be too late after you've hooked one, for there's nothing so sure that if you don't know where the snags are, the barbel does! A snag may not be in the immediate area of the swim, but a big and determined barbel will head for a snag ten or more yards from the swim given half a chance.

Landing Barbel

Barbel are long fish rather than a deep species like bream and carp, therefore you need a landing net that is big enough to cope with the length of them. The mesh should not be too fine or it will cause problems due to the often fast flow of a river pushing against it, especially considering you're going to have to handle the net with one hand while handling the rod with the other. The best procedure is to play the barbel to just upstream of the waiting net and

then use the rod and the flow of the current to carry the fish into the net. Once the fish is enclosed in the mesh you draw the net towards you, grasp the frame and lift the fish clear of the water. If the fish is not particularly notable, nowhere near a personal best, and not above a weight worth photographing, there is no reason why you cannot unhook it there and then and rest it in a quiet spot in the margins in the landing net to regain its strength before returning it. Stay with the fish while it's resting and don't be tempted to cast in again (if the resting area is close to your rod), for you may just hook another fish, which means you'll have to release the barbel you've already caught regardless of whether it's ready or not.

Unhooking and Weighing

Unhooking

If you've caught a barbel that is difficult to unhook in the landing net, or one you want to weigh, then you should carry the fish in the

Resting a barbel in the landing net before returning it is a safe way for it to recover.

A suitable pair of forceps makes short work of unhooking a barbel.

landing net to a pre-wetted unhooking mat, then lay it gently down in the net. Now carefully lift it from the net and place it on the mat as you move the net away. Very few barbel are hooked any deeper than just inside the lips, for the simple reason that they mouth a bait rather than suck it in, bolt off as soon as they feel the hook or line, and consequently rarely draw the hook deep into their mouth. So it is usually a simple job to grasp the hook with fingers and thumb, or with forceps (which should be placed ready and within easy reach of the mat), and remove it. A

large plastic disgorger is another alternative, and is often easier to use without damaging the knot whipping along the shank of the hook.

Once unhooked, check the fish for any wounds to the body or mouth damage (not necessarily inflicted by you) and if so, dab on a smear of Kryston Klin-Ik antiseptic solution.

Weighing and Returning
The fish should be placed in a wetted weigh sling, which has then been hung on the scales and the scales zeroed. While kneeling on the

Weigh a barbel over the unhooking mat for extra safety.

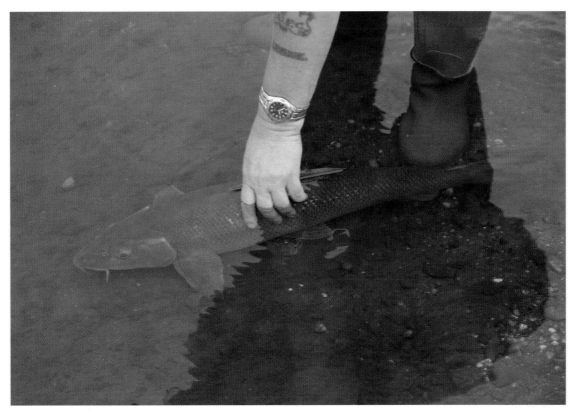

Patient nursing will ensure the barbel recovers completely before swimming off.

unhooking mat on which the fish rests enclosed in the weigh sling, carefully raise the scales by the handle provided until the weigh sling is just clear, and only just clear, of the unhooking mat. Read off the weight and carefully lower the weigh sling back to the unhooking mat. By following this procedure you ensure that if, for instance, the cord of the weigh sling broke, the fish would have a very short drop to the cushioned unhooking mat and would not suffer any injury.

The fish should then be taken to that quiet spot in the margins and held upright in the landing net until it has recovered enough to be released. Some anglers use a keepnet to retain the fish for just long enough for it to recover, but beware of fishery or club rules that ban the use of keepnets for barbel, and beware those who would not understand that the use of a keepnet for a single fish for a short spell is in the barbel's best interest.

Photography

It has become second nature, or at least a second hobby, for most specialist anglers to photograph their notable fish, and in this age of digital cameras it has never been easier. If you don't have anyone nearby to take the picture for you, you can use an adaptor on a bankstick as a camera support. But a tripod will give you a sturdier support, and can be used on hard ground where it would be difficult to drive in a bankstick to a sufficient depth to hold a camera steady enough, especially in a wind. The down side is that stable tripods are relatively heavy. There is now an answer, however, in the shape of the Gorillapod, which is a lightweight but sturdy three-legged camera support made from plastic, whose three legs can be bent to various shapes. It's only short, but cameras can be set to tilt upwards, and the Gorillapod can be attached to, for example, tree branches, fences and gates.

There a several ways in which you can set up to take a self-take photograph, the most popular one being a couple of banksticks at each end of the unhooking mat, on which you've pre-focused the camera from a pre-fixed position. Unless you've got a remote control or a bulb release you then set the camera timer and get between the banksticks with the fish and hope it doesn't move when the shutter is fired. Much of this procedure depends on what type of camera you have. The best for self-take shots are those cameras with a swivelling monitor, such as the Canon G11, with the monitor swivelled so that it faces away from the camera, allowing you to see yourself in it and know you and the fish are properly in shot. Couple this with a wireless remote and fire a burst of three shots and you have the ideal self-take set-up. The G11 also has a face recognition feature and almost guarantees you a good shot.

The Canon G11 camera, combined with a Gorillapod, has proved to be an ideal combination for self-take photos.

Having another angler on hand to do the photography can make things a lot easier.

13 BARBEL THROUGH THE CRYSTAL BALL

The Future of Barbel Fishing

The future of barbel and barbel fishing is uncertain, and while that may at first seem like a pessimistic outlook, it is in fact a good thing. Fishing itself is uncertain, for no one knows without a shadow of a doubt just what they're going to catch, if they catch at all, in any one day. It is this uncertainty, this vagueness, where success remains in doubt and dependent on so many factors you can do nothing about – the weather and water conditions, if the fish will feed – that makes fishing the fascinating sport it is.

Barbel have been called the 'second carp', meaning that the massive carp boom would be closely rivalled by a barbel boom, and indeed it has, at least to the point that river angling could be expected to rival it. That point was reached in the 2006 to 2008 seasons; since then it has been on the slide. Make no mistake, barbel have had some golden years, but none to match the last ten years when almost every notable barbel river was producing exceptional specimens. In 2004, the same year the barbel record topped 20lb for the first time with a fish from the Great Ouse, the River Dove began consistently to produce a string of mid-doubles from a stretch

Looking into a real crystal ball revealed Graham with a very big barbel – but is this what the future will hold?

ABOVE: It's likely we'll see more big barbel from big rivers like this Trent double caught by Bob Roberts. (Courtesy of Bob Roberts)

BELOW: It's possible that Grahame King will continue to hold the record for many years to come. (Courtesy of Grahame King)

where previously big singles and low doubles were hard to come by.

Many of the exceptional barbel being caught across the country were coming from small rivers such as those two, but even on the bigger rivers such as the Severn, the tidal Trent, the Ribble and the Thames, anglers were netting fish around the mid-teens of pounds, barbel far bigger than previously. No longer was barbel fishing mainly about fishing with a feeder, maggot or caster and hemp, for a bag of barbel in the 4–6lb bracket. The big boys had arrived with a vengeance, and everyone seemed to want a slice of the cake.

In 2006–07 the peak on the graph had hit an all-time high, with something like seventeen rivers producing the biggest barbel in their history; yet in 2008–09 it began to slide downhill, albeit slowly. In 2009 far fewer giant barbel were caught, and at the time the manuscript for this book was completed in 2010 we were suffering the harshest winter in many a year, with the whole country covered in snow for several weeks and prolonged temperatures hardly more than those normally found in polar regions. This will also have an impact on fish, including barbel, for they will have fed much less in winter than they normally do and therefore will not

This barbel shows evidence of predator damage to its tail, though we cannot be sure what caused it.

No matter if barbel sizes go up or down, they're all great to catch, just like this one being returned by Paul Williams.

have packed on the same average amount of weight as they have in the previous succession of wet and mild winters.

Yet there is always an upside, in that although the days of the huge 18lb-plus barbel, and the 20lb and over record breakers of Kickles Farm and Adams Mill on the Great Ouse, and Sayers Meadow on the Wensum, are over, at least for time being, the overall specimen barbel world will be better for it. It was an exciting time, particularly if you were there and fortunate enough to be able to fish those rivers, but for the rest of us, it made our low doubles seem like tiddlers and not fit to grace the pages of our angling weeklies. You can't blame the papers for that – they only print the news, they don't make it – and a twelve-pounder from the Trent, a huge fish for the river, doesn't compare in newsworthy terms to an eighteen-pounder from the Great Ouse. In reality it did, of course, in terms of size for the river, but in headline terms there was no contest.

So at least for the near future, barbel fishing will be back to something like normal. There will still be rivers producing significantly bigger barbel than most other rivers, but at least the biggest fish will not seem so much like aliens from another planet. All species go through cycles, with peaks and troughs on the growth rate graph, and you never know when there will be a climatic event, or an increase in predators such as otters, mink and cormorants, which changes the usual trend quite dramatically. It is easy enough to lay the blame on otters, mink and cormorants, and no doubt they carry part of the blame; but it is as well to remember that it is the bigger barbel that disappeared from the Great Ouse and the Wensum, and the biggest are usually the oldest, so we can expect some natural fatalities through old age. It won't come as any surprise to these authors if the ultimate average size of barbel has now settled to a more realistic figure and stabilizes around that figure – for a few years at least.

Another factor is that it has been noticeable for the last few years, on most rivers anyhow, that smaller barbel, those up to 5lb or so, are slowly disappearing. It is true to say that on most notable barbel rivers it is now easier to catch an 8lb or bigger barbel than one of 4lb or less. Indeed, on many notable barbel rivers it is easier to catch a double than a small one. This is worrying, because although barbel specialists don't want to catch small barbel, the sensible ones realize that it is the smaller ones that are the future. If there are no generations of barbel coming through, then the barbel future looks barren. Yet although a somewhat dismal picture has been painted, we don't expect anything too drastic. What is likely to happen is that the species will continue to settle and stabilize, and will eventually fit in better with other, longer established species such as chub, dace and roach, rather than continuing to be the dominant species on some rivers.

Future growth rates will be greatly influenced by the type of winters we have. If we experience a return to the wet and warm winters of the golden years, then growth rates will soar again, although perhaps not to the same extent as previously. If we get more winters like the present one of 2009/2010, then the growth rate could decelerate even further.

Yet another factor is that the EA are tending to stock more barbel from their Calverton fish farm where they are being bred under ideal conditions, so no matter how much stocks may become depleted, there is always the likelihood that they will be replaced via the fish farm route.

Stillwater Barbel

There is no doubt that this is a controversial subject, for there are many dedicated barbel anglers who think that barbel do not belong in stillwaters, that they are a species with a biology and body shape that is meant for flowing water only. Our foremost barbel organization, the Barbel Society, has this to say:

> The Barbel Society remains resolutely opposed to the stocking of barbel in stillwaters. The barbel is clearly highly adapted to life in flowing water with consistently low temperatures and high oxygen levels, and requires great care on return to the water after capture. There is little evidence that barbel already stocked into stillwaters thrive or survive in the long term, or that there is a strong or genuine demand from anglers for stillwater barbel. The Society urges fishery owners to refrain from stocking barbel into stillwaters, and also expects the Environment Agency to review their policy of allowing such stockings. The moral and ethical arguments against stillwater barbel are also considerable. Putting barbel into lakes is like keeping kestrels in a chicken coop.

One can sympathize with the Barbel Society, and anyone else who puts barbel on a pedestal to be worshipped and revered. You can find the same narrow-minded view with any single-species group regarding their particular species. It's not wrong, but the ethos does close the door on any meaningful and open-minded debate on any controversial topic concerning 'their' species.

Stillwater barbel are not a recent occurrence, and they have been swimming wild and swimming free in stillwaters since barbel have been in rivers, because excessive floodwater ensures that when the river overflows it carries fish to nearby pools and lakes. Those with long memories will remember the exploits of Peter Rayment catching barbel from Trimpley Reservoir back in the

Graham's grandson Calum caught this stillwater barbel.

1960s and 1970s. He later wrote an excellent chapter on the subject in *Barbel* by the Barbel Catchers and Friends. In this chapter, he outlines the long history of barbel being able to thrive in Stillwater, and listed about fifteen stillwaters known to hold barbel at that time (1988). In most cases, the barbel had been able to colonize the lake concerned through some link to a nearby river, whether by flooding or a stream connection. It is clear that his view was that barbel had no great difficulty in thriving in stillwater provided the water was suitable. In some cases, the growth rate was better in a stillwater than in a river, to which some of the barbel were subsequently transferred. Evidence of barbel spawning was inconclusive, though cited in one or two instances.

The recent debates have centred on the stocking of the modern commercial fisheries with barbel. Some, indeed most, of these stockings have been carried out by the EA using Calverton fish. Other stockings are much more controversial, because adult fish up to 10lb or more have suddenly appeared in lakes. One of the main objections to the stocking of barbel into these waters has been the generally high stock densities that prevail, as well as the heavy fishing pressure.

There are several arguments that are being used against stocking barbel into stillwaters. The first is that barbel evolved as a flowing water fish. This is essentially true, and so far there is virtually no evidence that barbel are able to spawn successfully in stillwater. But how essential is fast flowing water for barbel to thrive past fingerling size? Second, it is argued that stillwaters, especially heavily stocked ones, cannot provide a suitable habitat. Surely, the opponents of these stockings argue, the water temperature will be too high in summer, dissolved oxygen levels too low, the whole environment too stressful. The other objections are that the pools will

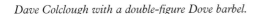

Dave Colclough with a double-figure Dove barbel.

be heavily match-fished and the barbel retained in keepnets, and that the whole environment is so far removed from wild and beautiful rivers that it is an insult to do this to so noble a fish. Some studies have shown that river barbel are fitter than stillwater barbel, and of course it will be essential to sustain a stillwater population of barbel through restocking.

One indicator of fish habitat suitability must be growth rates and condition. As Peter Rayment explained, barbel growth rates in stillwater have been proved comparable with those achieved in flowing water. If this were not the case one would expect stocked adult fish to lose condition and die, but the converse appears to occur. The growth rates that Rayment found would probably differ significantly in favour of the river fish nowadays. It could be said that in some instances stillwater barbel are better suited to heavily stocked stillwaters than are some species that are often found there, which doesn't upset anyone. Bream and roach often struggle in these conditions, as they are intolerant of heavy match-fishing pressure. Mark recalls:

Many years ago I fished a summer match on the Thames at Carrot's Ham above Oxford. The river barely moved. I was amazed to see one angler weigh in a barbel (only about 3lb) from a deep bend. The river was to all intents and purposes a Stillwater, yet here was a barbel swim, for the swim was noted for them. My preconceptions of fast water being required to support them evaporated. A year later, I watched the barbel spawning at Wolvercote, Oxford (where Peter Stone lived). There were hundreds of them, yet these fish spent the rest of the year in the sluggish Medley Reach. Perhaps barbel are far more tolerant of stillwater than some would have us believe.

So we are left with an inconclusive debate. On the one hand it can be said that barbel are not by nature a stillwater fish and do not readily spawn in stillwater, but on the other hand they will indeed thrive and live apparently healthy lives in clean stillwaters that are not overstocked and heavily match-fished. Isn't the latter evidently true of all species? It will come as no surprise to anyone if a new British record barbel was one day captured from a stillwater, a stillwater that is already understocked with very large carp and being fished regularly by carp anglers who are feeding highly nutritious baits.

In the next decade or so, these authors expect barbel to become a popular and widely accepted stillwater species.

A prolific barbel stretch of the River Dove in winter.

BIBLIOGRAPHY AND USEFUL INFORMATION

This list is far from complete, but it does include the major titles plus a few classics. Many of the small run, self-published books have been left out, mainly because they are out of print and you are unlikely to find them.

Arbery, Len *The Complete Book of River Fishing* (David & Charles, 1993).

Baker, John *Modern Barbel Baits and Tactics* (John Baker Products, 2005).

Barbel Catchers and Friends *Barbel* (The Crowood Press, 1998).

Barbel Catchers *Barbel Rivers and Captures* (The Crowood Press, 2004).

Berry, Jon *A Can of Worms* (Medlar, 2007).

Church, Bob (ed.) *Big Barbel: Bonded by the Challenge* (The Crowood Press, 2005).

Crouch, Fred *Understanding Barbel* (Beekay, 1986).

Giles, Nick *The Nature of Barbel* (The Minster Press, 2002).

Miles, Tony *Elite Barbel* (Little Egret, 2004).

Miles, Tony and West, Trefor *Quest For Barbel* (The Crowood Press, 1991).

Miller, Roger *The Complete Barbel Angler* (The Crowood Press, 1996).

Orme, Andy *Barbel Mania* (The Crowood Press, 1990).

Orme, Andy *Roving for Barbel: Parts 1 & 2* (Seer Rods, 1999).

Searl, John *A Brush with the Avon* (The Art of Angling, 2007).

Stone, Peter *Bream and Barbel* (EMAP, 1963).

West, Trefor *Barbel: A Lifetime's Addiction* (Whacked It Publications, 2005).

Wheat, Peter *The Fighting Barbel* (Ernest Benn, 1967).

Wilson, John *Catch Barbel with John Wilson* (Boxtree, 1992).

Yates, Chris *The River Prince* (Medlar, 1998, 2009).

Yates, Chris *River Diaries* (Medlar, 1997).

Yates, Chris *The Deepening Pool* (Unwin & Hyman, 1990).

Useful Contacts

A quick Google of the internet should reveal a number of useful sites for the barbel angler; here are some of them:

www.thebarbelsociety.co.uk
www.barbelcatchersclub.co.uk
www.barbel.co.uk
www.barbelnow.co.uk
www.barbel-fishing.me.uk
www.anglingtrust.net
www.fishingmagic.com
www.anglersnet.co.uk

INDEX